10 Minutes to Beat Anxiety and Panic

also in the 10 Minutes to Better Mental Health series

10 Minutes to Better Mental Health
A Step-by-Step Guide for Teens Using CBT and Mindfulness
Lee David and Debbie Brewin
Illustrated by Rebecca Price
ISBN 978 1 78775 556 7
eISBN 978 1 78775 570 3

of related interest

Free From Panic
A Teen's Guide to Coping with Panic Attacks and Panic Symptoms
Monika Parkinson, Kerstin Thirlwall and Lucy Willetts
Illustrated by Richy. K Chandler
ISBN 978 1 78775 818 6
eISBN 978 1 78775 819 3

My Anxiety Handbook
Getting Back on Track
Sue Knowles, Bridie Gallagher and Phoebe McEwen
Illustrated by Emmeline Pidgen
ISBN 978 1 78592 440 8
eISBN 978 1 78450 813 5

10 minutes TO BEAT ANXIETY AND PANIC

A Step-by-Step Guide for Teens Using CBT and Mindfulness

Lee David and Debbie Brewin

Illustrated by Rebecca Price

Jessica Kingsley Publishers
London and Philadelphia

First published in Great Britain in 2025 by Jessica Kingsley Publishers
An imprint of John Murray Press

1

Copyright © Lee David and Debbie Brewin 2025
Illustration copyright © Rebecca Price 2025

The right of Lee David and Debbie Brewin to be identified as the Authors of the Work has
been asserted by them in accordance with the Copyright, Designs and Patents Act 1988.

Front cover image source: iStockphoto®. The cover image is for illustrative
purposes only, and any person featuring is a model.

This book is intended to convey information to the reader. It is not intended
for medical diagnosis or treatment. The reader should seek appropriate
professional care and attention for any specific healthcare needs.

A CIP catalogue record for this title is available from the British Library and the Library of Congress

ISBN 978 1 83997 848 7
eISBN 978 1 83997 849 4

Printed and bound in Great Britain by Bell & Bain Limited

Jessica Kingsley Publishers' policy is to use papers that are natural, renewable and recyclable
products and made from wood grown in sustainable forests. The logging and manufacturing
processes are expected to conform to the environmental regulations of the country of origin.

Jessica Kingsley Publishers
Carmelite House
50 Victoria Embankment
London EC4Y 0DZ

www.jkp.com

John Murray Press
Part of Hodder & Stoughton Limited
An Hachette UK Company

The authorised representative in the EEA is Hachette Ireland,
8 Castlecourt Centre, Dublin 15, D15 XTP3, Ireland (email: info@hbgi.ie)

Contents

Introduction

→ Are you constantly anxious, tense or worried, and is it hard to feel calm or relaxed?

→ Does your mind always jump to the scariest or most embarrassing possibilities?

→ Is anxiety keeping you stuck in a rut, unable to take risks or live your life for fear that things might go wrong?

→ Have you got 10 minutes? Keep reading to find out how to free yourself from fear and worry.

Erin: My anxiety could just come out of nowhere. I'd start out feeling jittery and a bit sick, with sweaty palms. Then I would feel my heart beginning to thump in my chest. I started throwing up in the morning at the thought of going to school. The feelings were so strong it seemed like there must be something really wrong with me. I didn't know about anxiety and I couldn't understand why I kept reacting like this. I just wanted it to stop!

Pranav: Even since I was young, I always used to worry about things. I remember lying awake in bed worrying that someone in my family would get cancer. If anyone was out of the house, I would think that they might be in a car accident or even kidnapped. I can spend ages thinking over and over again about all the things that might go wrong. I get stuck in my thoughts and can't seem to move past my worries. It's hard to concentrate on my schoolwork or to relax and enjoy my free time.

What is anxiety?

Anxiety is the feeling you get when you're worried or scared about something. It's normal to feel anxious or worried from time to time. Maybe you are facing a new challenge or a change, such as moving house or school, or there may be pressures to pass exams or perform in front of others. Often, feelings of anxiety are short-lived and will pass once you have come through a challenging situation.

But sometimes anxiety can become a bigger problem. You might have stronger or more frequent feelings of fear, worry or dread, which may become overwhelming and harder to manage. You might find that anxiety stops you from being able to live your life and do the things you normally enjoy because you have lost confidence, or you avoid situations or people that might make you feel anxious.

If that's true for you, then it's time to take action and find ways to deal with your anxiety.

Throughout this book, we will share many examples like Erin's and Pranav's above and discover how they learned to cope with different types of anxiety.

The growing problem of anxiety

Anxiety is one of the most common mental health challenges experienced by young people, and it can lead to problems with friendships, family life and education. Anxiety often starts in childhood and, if unchecked, can have a major impact throughout adult life.

The numbers are growing. In a recent survey, 56 per cent of young people reported always or often feeling anxious (Prince's Trust Tesco Youth Index 2021)**.** This has been made worse by the increased stress, social isolation and disruption brought on by the Covid-19 pandemic.

Different types of anxiety

In this book, we will explore ways to understand and cope with many types of anxiety. If anxiety is affecting you, we recommend that you talk to a trusted adult or visit your doctor for advice. Anxiety can be successfully treated, especially when it is picked up early.

Anxiety can show up in many different ways. We will explore ways to understand and cope with all these different types of anxiety as we continue through this book.

Panic attacks

A panic attack is a short episode of severe anxiety which usually comes on quickly and lasts up to around 20 minutes. There are intense feelings of fear and strong physical reactions such as tightness or pain in the chest, sweating or dizziness. This can lead to avoidance of activities that you fear may trigger a panic attack, which can have a major impact on daily life.

Generalized anxiety disorder

People with generalized anxiety disorder worry about many different situations and life problems. The worry is out of proportion to the problems and involves repeated loops of thinking about the same issues. Worry often also affects the body, causing tiredness, headaches, muscle tension and difficulty sleeping.

Social anxiety

People who suffer from social anxiety become fearful in social or performance situations such as speaking or eating in public, going to parties, performing in front of others or talking to new or unfamiliar people. They may worry about appearing nervous or about making mistakes that mean they will be judged or rejected by others.

Health anxiety

This involves intense fear and worry about having a serious illness, which can continue even if you have seen medical professionals. You may find yourself repeatedly checking your body for new symptoms or looking up health issues online. You might also find yourself asking friends and family for reassurance or attending health clinics frequently. This can help for a while, but the anxiety often comes back soon afterwards.

Take action about your anxiety

Anxiety is common, yet as many as two-thirds of young people with anxiety do not reach out and seek professional help or support. Without treatment, this can lead to long-term anxiety problems that last through adult life, as well as other difficulties including depression, use of alcohol or drugs, problems with education and achievement, and even self-harm and suicide.

It is important to recognize if you are living with anxiety and to seek help, especially if it is starting to affect your everyday life.

The good news is that you can learn to cope with anxiety and live a happy and fulfilled life even if anxiety sometimes pays you a visit. Anxiety is one of the most treatable mental health conditions. You can learn to retrain your brain and change your 'anxiety habits' into new and helpful ways of coping with anything that life throws at you.

Talking to someone that you trust, such as a teacher, parent or health professional about your anxiety can help you to make sense of what you are going through and help you make choices and decisions about how best to cope.

How can this book help?

This book is a practical toolkit which includes information, exercises, tips and skills to help you understand and deal with anxiety. We've broken it down into bite-sized chunks which take only 10 minutes a day to overcome anxiety and improve your confidence to do the things in life that are most important to you.

The book is based on effective treatments for anxiety including cognitive behavioural therapy (CBT), which looks at making changes in how you think, feel and behave when you are feeling anxious. Research shows that CBT is a highly successful treatment for anxiety in young people and adults (James *et al.* 2020; van Dis *et al.* 2020).

We also use simple and quick tools based on mindfulness to help you step back from anxious thoughts and feelings and feel less overwhelmed and better able to cope.

This book will help you to:

→ notice when anxiety pops up and learn to recognize when it's just a false alarm and you are actually safe and sound

→ stop anxiety from getting in the way of living the life that you want to lead

→ become more present and focused on the here and now, rather than caught up in worries about things that might go wrong in the future

→ cope better with strong or overwhelming emotions such as anxiety, fear and panic

→ build your confidence and motivate yourself to achieve the things that you care most about.

What will we cover in this book?

The book is divided into three sections:

Part 1 – Understanding anxiety and panic: In this section, we will learn more about what anxiety is, how to recognize it and the different ways it can affect your body, emotions, thoughts and behaviour.

Part 2 – Different types of anxiety: In this section, we will look at some of the common types of anxiety, including learning more about:

→ dealing with stressful life situations

→ panic attacks

→ coping with worry

→ shyness and social anxiety

→ health anxiety.

You might choose to read all these chapters to get a better understanding of different types of anxiety, or you might prefer to focus on the chapters that feel most relevant to you.

Part 3 – 10 Minute GROWTH steps for overcoming anxiety: This final section will look at six key skills that will help you beat anxiety and create healthy habits. You can use these steps whenever you face a difficult situation, helping you to build your confidence and stop anxiety from limiting how you live your life.

Here is a quick overview of the steps that we'll be exploring in this section:

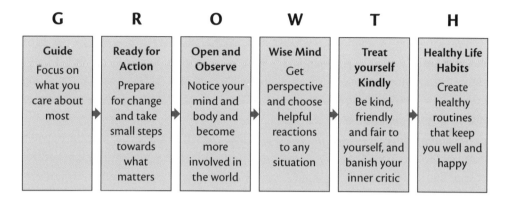

G	**R**	**O**	**W**	**T**	**H**
Guide Focus on what you care about most	**Ready for Action** Prepare for change and take small steps towards what matters	**Open and Observe** Notice your mind and body and become more involved in the world	**Wise Mind** Get perspective and choose helpful reactions to any situation	**Treat yourself Kindly** Be kind, friendly and fair to yourself, and banish your inner critic	**Healthy Life Habits** Create healthy routines that keep you well and happy

Read This   10 Minutes

How to get the most out of this book

We have made the book as interactive as possible. Each chapter includes sections where you will be invited to do the following:

→ **Read This:** Background information and explanations to make sense of what happens when you feel low or depressed, and ways to overcome those feelings.

→ **Pause and Think:** There are many opportunities for you to stop and think about how things are affecting you personally.

→ **Do This:** We've included lots of practical ideas and activities you can carry out to practise skills in your own life.

We've also included space in the book to keep a note of your thoughts. Writing things down can help you see things differently, remember helpful insights and encourage you to commit to trying something new. Look out for the pencil icon for opportunities to try this out.

The book also includes many examples of young people who are finding ways to understand and overcome their own struggles with anxiety. The characters are fictional, but the examples have been developed and inspired by our experiences of working with real individuals over many years.

Building new habits

Change can be difficult and, at first, it might seem more comfortable to stick with what you know. Imagine you are walking on a path through a forest. It often feels easier and safer to take the route that you know well and have taken many times before. However, what if this well-worn route becomes a rut and involves habits and actions that stop you from seeing other interesting things and may actually worsen your anxiety over time?

We are going to encourage you to start taking small steps away from the path that you usually choose. It might feel a little scary to go a different way, but it's also an opportunity to explore, learn more about yourself and discover new and exciting things in life. Remember, you only have to take small steps and build your confidence gradually from each success.

As you practise new ways of reacting to life stresses and difficult situations, you'll start to reap the rewards as you see progress. You will find that anxiety is less in control of your life, and you are increasingly confident to do the things that are most important to you.

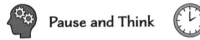 **Pause and Think**  **5 Minutes**

How is anxiety affecting your life?

Take a few minutes to think about the ways that anxiety is affecting you now. This can help you to understand yourself better and motivate you to start to make changes in how you deal with anxiety.

How is anxiety affecting you and your life?	
What are you missing out on because you struggle with anxiety? Have you stopped doing something because you have lost confidence? Are you avoiding people or places so you don't feel anxious?	
How would life be different or better if you were not coping with anxiety?	
What activities would you do more of if you had more confidence?	

Pranav completed the activity. Here are his answers.

How is anxiety affecting you and your life?	*I have constant worries about things that might go wrong. I spend so much of my time trying to control my anxiety or stop myself getting anxious, it feels like it has taken over my life and I feel fed up and stuck.*
What are you missing out on because you struggle with anxiety? Have you stopped doing something because you have lost confidence? Are you avoiding people or places so you don't feel anxious?	*I've become cut off from my friends and I no longer do many of my hobbies because I've lost so much confidence. I spend more time by myself at home, which can be quite lonely.*
How would life be different or better if you were not coping with anxiety?	*If I felt less anxious, I would be able to enjoy my life more. I would spend more time with my friends and have more fun. I would do more activities in my free time and spend less time worrying.*
What activities would you do more of if you had more confidence?	*I would play badminton at weekends again. I might even try to get a summer job.*

Summary

→ You can take practical steps to overcome anxiety with help and support.

→ This book draws on effective treatments for anxiety such as CBT and mindfulness.

→ You will get the most out of this book if you try out the exercises in your life to find out what works best for you.

Final thoughts
Make a note of anything you have found helpful, interesting or surprising in this chapter.

....

....

....

....

....

....

What are you going to do now? Can you choose one small action for the coming week based on what you have read so far? Can you commit to reading this book and spending time on yourself for 10 minutes each day? Anything else?

....

....

....

....

....

....

Part 1

UNDERSTANDING ANXIETY AND PANIC

Chapter 1

WHAT IS ANXIETY?

Amina: For the first few months of having anxiety, I thought I was going crazy. Sometimes I even thought I was dying. It got so bad that I stopped going out and seeing my friends. I could hardly get to college without having a panic attack. My sleep was bad and I was tired and snappy with my family and friends. I had no one I could talk to who understood and I began to feel hopeless and depressed.

Evan: Anxiety mainly used to affect my body. I felt restless and I couldn't keep still. My legs would shake and I felt like I had to lie down or I might pass out. I had tummy aches and my head would throb. It was really hard to concentrate.

Anxiety is common, but it can be a lonely and scary experience if you don't understand what's happening to you.

The first step towards overcoming anxiety is to learn more about it. So, in this chapter, we will:

→ learn how to recognize feelings of anxiety

→ discover what anxiety is and why we get it

→ meet your Anxiety Alarm system and learn how it helps keep you safe from danger

→ find out what happens in your body when you start to feel anxious.

 Read This   5 Minutes

Recognizing anxiety and panic

Everyone feels anxious at times, and it can even be useful. The nervousness and fear that arise before sitting an exam or giving a performance can keep your mind focused, encourage you to prepare and motivate you to do your best to rise to the occasion.

It's common to feel anxious when you are coping with problems or stressful life situations. You might have worries about friendships, money or health, or when under stress like at exam time. This type of anxiety is usually short-lived and will often pass once the difficult situation is over.

For some people, feelings of fear and worry can last longer or may appear even when you are not in a stressful situation. You may develop an 'anxiety habit' where you tend to over-estimate problems and risks, so you feel anxious more often or more strongly than you need to. You might also become stuck doing things repeatedly to prevent or avoid anxiety, which can get in the way of living an enjoyable life.

 Pause and Think    5 Minutes

Are you feeling anxious?

It's important to spot when you are struggling with feelings and emotions that may be due to anxiety. This will help you to choose more helpful ways to react when they appear.

Complete the following checklist which will explore some of the common feelings you might notice if you are experiencing anxiety.

Over the past two weeks, have you been affected often or very often by the following feelings?	Tick if you have noticed this
Nervousness or worry	
Unease or uncertainty	
Stress or tension	
Panic or terror	
Overwhelm	
Irritability or anger	
A sense of dread	

Pause and Think **10 Minutes**

What causes anxiety?

There are many different reasons for anxiety and panic. Look at the list below. Are any of these issues affecting you at the moment?

Cause of anxiety	Examples	Is this happening in your life? What examples can you think of?
Life stresses and problems	Problems such as being bullied, money worries, moving away from friends and coping with pressure and expectations, including exams and coursework, can all cause anxiety. We talk about this more in Chapter 5.	
Past experiences	Traumatic or upsetting events in the past can make you more likely to feel anxious or panicky. These include scary events like an accident or serious injury, distressing experiences of abuse or neglect, or the loss of a friend or family member.	
Your health	Health problems such as diabetes or asthma may make you more at risk of anxiety. Other conditions such as an overactive thyroid can cause symptoms that are similar to anxiety. If you are worried about your physical health, we advise seeing your doctor to check if there is a medical cause for your anxiety.	
Body changes	Certain foods, caffeine, alcohol and drugs can affect your body and cause anxiety. Teenagers and young adults will also go through a period of tremendous growth and development which can affect your body and brain in many ways.	

cont.

Cause of anxiety	Examples	Is this happening in your life? What examples can you think of?
Your development	Anxiety may be more common in young people with developmental challenges or neurodivergence such as autism, ADHD or dyslexia.	
Your personality	Some personality traits may make you more prone to anxiety such as being timid, a perfectionist, disliking change and being introverted or shy.	
Family and genetics	Having a close relative with anxiety can increase your chances of developing it yourself. This may be a combination of inherited tendencies and learned behaviour from the people around you.	

Everyone is different and there may be a complicated mix of reasons for your anxiety, which are not always clear-cut. The good news is that even if you are not sure why you are anxious, or if some life problems are difficult to change or are outside your control, you can still find ways to deal with any anxiety that is causing you difficulties.

Anxiety and your Threat system

You experience anxiety when your body's inner **Threat system** is activated. This is your in-built survival system. It's there to keep you alive and safe when you are in immediate danger.

When your Threat system detects any potential dangers, it sends alert messages to your brain. By releasing hormones such as adrenaline and cortisol, it tells your body to take rapid action that will keep you safe. You don't even have to think about it – your body takes over and reacts automatically and quickly.

Pause and Think **5 Minutes**

Imagine you are walking down a quiet street. You turn a corner and suddenly you are faced by a bear! The bear stands up on its hind legs and growls at you!

→ How might you react?

→ What would you need to do to get away safely?

→ What sensations might you feel in your body?

Amina says: If I was faced by a bear, I would feel terrified! My heart would be thumping in my chest. At first, I would probably freeze and I wouldn't know what to do. But then I think I would run! When I got away, I would be panting for breath and feel very shaky.

 Read This **10 Minutes**

Why do we need anxiety?

The Threat system is controlled by a part of the brain that has been present since early humans had to fend off wild animals to survive. By triggering anxiety, it helps your body to react quickly to danger.

The body reactions that enable this to happen are known as **Fight Flight Freeze**. To stay safe, you have to **Fight** off anything that is threatening, take **Flight** and run away to escape a dangerous situation or **Freeze**, staying completely still so that you avoid detection. If you are in danger, anxiety is protective and makes sure you stay alive!

The Threat system is often alert in the background, looking out for potential danger. It's important to act quickly when you are under threat as there isn't much time to think or plan what to do. So, this system can be triggered rapidly when your brain thinks you are facing any kind of risk.

Physical changes in anxiety

The Fight Flight Freeze reaction is controlled by the part of your brain called the **brainstem** and a system of nerves that runs throughout the body called the **sympathetic nervous system**. The hormone adrenaline is released and leads to many physical changes which help you deal with threats and dangers. We've summarized the common body reactions to anxiety in the diagram below:

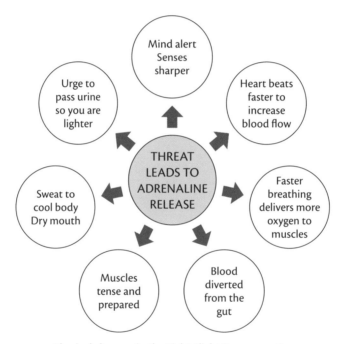

Physical changes in the Fight Flight Freeze reaction

Think back to the example where you suddenly meet a bear in the street.

Because of your body's Fight Flight Freeze reactions, you can run away, fight it off or stay completely still so that the bear ignores you and leaves you alone. You've survived! So, in this situation, the Threat system and the automatic body changes were necessary and helpful.

But the surge of hormones and body reactions that are triggered when your Threat system is activated can be intense and cause uncomfortable sensations. You may get blurred vision, muffled ears, breathlessness, feel sick or dizzy and be unable to move or think clearly, and your brain may start to worry that something is seriously wrong with your health!

It is important to recognize that these body sensations of anxiety are *not* dangerous, even though they may be unpleasant. They are *normal* reactions to anything that seems like a threat and will gradually fade away once the danger has passed. Understanding this can be the first step in coping with anxiety.

 Pause and Think  **5 Minutes**

Body changes during anxiety

Complete the following checklist which includes many of the common body changes you might notice when you are experiencing anxiety or panic.

Over the past two weeks, have you been affected often or very often by the following body changes?	Tick if you have noticed this
Trouble getting to sleep or waking in the night	
Feeling jumpy, fidgety or easily startled	
Finding it hard to concentrate	
Feeling light-headed, faint or dizzy	
Heart beating fast or thumping in your chest	
Dry mouth, sweating or feeling hot	
Frequent or repeated nightmares	
Tightness or discomfort in your chest, changes to your breathing	
Shakiness or trembling, wobbly legs	
Blurred vision or a ringing in your ears	
Frequent headaches or migraines	
Butterflies, tummy pains, bloating or feeling sick	
Muscle aches and pains	
Lack of appetite	
Feeling more tired than usual	

Evan says: I hadn't realized how many ways anxiety can affect my body! I thought there was something wrong with me. Doing this checklist of body changes has helped me to understand that what I'm feeling is anxiety. I still get the feelings – sometimes I wake up with my heart racing or I feel shaky and dizzy and have tummy aches. But knowing that these are all due to anxiety means I don't feel so helpless and worried.

 **Read This**  **10 Minutes**

The Anxiety Alarm system

Just like a smoke alarm, anxiety is an important system that alerts you and helps you take action in the face of threat and danger. If there is a fire, you want the alarm to alert you early, so that you can put it out. But you don't want the smoke alarm going off as soon as your toast starts to brown, way before it gets burnt!

Likewise, it's helpful to have an Anxiety Alarm that's roughly in proportion to the threat – so you can trust it to help get you out of danger when needed but with few unnecessary false alarms.

If you over-estimate or exaggerate dangers and threats in your mind, then you may develop a super-sensitive Threat system that triggers anxiety even when situations are not really dangerous. Other people find it hard to stop worrying or their body feels tense or 'wired' even after the danger has passed. This is like a smoke alarm that's hard to turn off once it starts beeping.

Even if there are a few false alarms, you don't want to throw your Anxiety Alarm in the bin because it is designed to keep you safe when there is a major problem to deal with. However, you can learn to notice when it goes off, check quickly for danger and then switch it off and continue with your day without letting it affect you for too long.

And if on some days it goes off a bit too often, it's not the worst thing, especially if you understand more about anxiety and how it affects your body.

Pause and Think **5 Minutes**

Take a few minutes to answer the following questions:

Why do we need an Anxiety Alarm? How can it help us in the modern world? E.g.: *Because there are still some dangers and it's important to stay safe.*	
What do you notice first when your alarm system goes off? E.g.: *I jump at any loud noise.*	
What sort of situations, people and places usually set off your alarm system? E.g.: *When I'm at school and have a maths lesson that I can't understand.*	
Can you switch your alarm back off again? How do you do this? E.g.: *I ask a teacher or my friend for help.*	
Does it sometimes go on for longer or spiral out of control? What happens? E.g.: *I can't sit still or concentrate, and I start to worry about lots of things.*	

 Read This **5 Minutes**

Your amazing imagination

Your incredible brain can imagine risks, problems and dangers before they happen. This is extremely helpful for being able to predict difficulties, make plans and stop yourself getting into trouble.

However, if you have an inventive brain that tends to dwell on problems, or a brain that over-estimates risks and always thinks about the worst-case scenario, this can trigger your Anxiety Alarm unnecessarily. Spending a lot of time with your Threat system acti-vated can make you feel edgy, jumpy and unable to relax and can get in the way of memory, learning and relaxation.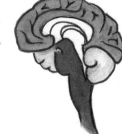

Your Anxiety Alarm is triggered in exactly the same way regard-less if the threat is real or imagined. So, a real threat such as facing a bear in the street will trigger the same physical reactions as worrying about something that might never actually happen.

We will look in more detail at how your mind and your thoughts can trigger anxiety in Chapter 2.

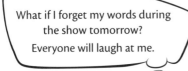

 Do This **3 Minutes**

Notice the NOW and manage your Anxiety Alarm

Next time you are starting to feel stressed or tense, take a few minutes to **Notice the NOW**. This simple and quick exercise can help to settle your anxiety and allow you to recognize that your activated Threat system may be just a false alarm and you're actually safe and sound.

There are three steps:

1. **N**otice and name your thoughts and feelings: *I'm worrying about the argument with my friend. I'm thinking about the essay I have to write. My tummy and my chest feel tight. My hands are shaking. I notice that I'm feeling anxious and tense.*

2. **O**bserve your body and the world around you: *I can feel my feet on the floor. I'm lying on my bed and I can feel the soft mattress underneath me. I can see a bird flying outside the window. I can hear the noise of people talking in the next room.*

3. **W**hat matters? Decide what's most important for you to focus on and then move on to do this with your full attention. *It's important for me to concentrate on my homework. I'm talking to my friend and I want to listen to him properly rather than getting distracted by my worries.*

We will introduce many more skills for balancing your Threat system and coping with feelings of anxiety as we continue through this book.

Amina says: It's been helpful to read about all the ways that anxiety can affect my body and emotions. Once I could understand what was going on, I began opening up to my friends and family about how I was feeling. They were supportive, and several of my friends shared that they had anxiety too. I stopped feeling so alone and it gave me some confidence to start to deal with my worries.

Summary: what is anxiety?

→ Anxiety can cause many emotions including feeling uneasy, tense, panicky or irritable.

→ The Threat system was developed to keep you safe from danger by triggering the Fight Flight Freeze reaction.

→ When the Anxiety Alarm is activated, you may notice many body reactions such as feeling jumpy, faint, dizzy, having a rapid heart rate, shakiness or fast breathing.

→ Your Threat system reacts in the same way to real and imagined threats and can be triggered by worries that are unlikely to ever happen.

Final thoughts

Make a note of anything you have found helpful, interesting or surprising from this chapter.

....

....

....

....

....

....

....

What are you going to do now? Can you choose one small action for the coming week based on what you have read so far?

....

....

....

....

....

....

....

Chapter 2

YOUR ANXIOUS MIND

Maya: Sometimes I wake up in the night worrying and I can't switch the thoughts off. It's like my mind starts spiralling out of control. I have this 'what if...?' voice that always jumps straight to the worst thing that could happen, which makes me really stressed and panicky. I keep telling myself that the things I'm thinking about are not true, and I try to tell myself to snap out of it, but I can still spend hours going over and over the same silly things.

Rory: I've just got through my first week of college and I was anxious the whole time. Even though I haven't done anything wrong or made any mistakes, I keep thinking that I'm not going to be able to cope in my classes and I won't be able to make any friends. I walked through the corridors keeping my eyes on the ground, trying not to look like a complete loser. Inside I just kept thinking how I'm bound to say something stupid and mess things up or look like an idiot in front of the teachers and other students.

 Read This  5 Minutes

Anxious thinking habits

Since developing language, humans have used this amazing ability to talk and think about problems verbally. We can also use our thinking brain to imagine danger and plan how to solve it. You don't have to fall off a cliff to know it's dangerous! You can use your incredible mind to imagine what might happen and avoid it before you injure yourself.

This is a hugely important tool for solving practical problems, but it also means that you can *imagine* problems, exaggerate them and become anxious about things that are not likely to happen in real life. As we learned in the last chapter, your Anxiety Alarm triggers the Threat system in the exact same way for real danger as for problems that are invented by our creative anxious brains.

In this chapter, we will:

→ explore how anxiety can change the way you look at the world

→ learn about the common thoughts that can appear when you become anxious

→ learn how getting stuck on the 'Anxiety Train' in your mind can keep you trapped and feeling fearful

→ meet some of the passengers who might jump onto your Anxiety Train and set off your Anxiety Alarm.

 Pause and Think **5 Minutes**

Do you have anxious thinking habits?

People who are more prone to becoming anxious often have ways of thinking about the world that trigger the Threat system and switch on the Anxiety Alarm.

Complete the following checklist which includes some of the common ways of thinking that can trigger anxiety.

Over the past two weeks, have you noticed the following ways of thinking often or very often?	Tick if you have noticed this
Do you worry about future problems that may never happen?	
Does your brain exaggerate the risks or possible things that might go wrong?	
Do you lack confidence in your ability to cope with problems, and forget or discount your abilities and past successes?	
Do you find it difficult to cope with uncertainty, and want to feel sure what's going to happen in the future?	
Do you think that worrying about problems can help keep you safe and stop the worst from happening?	
Do you think in extreme ways, such as assuming that things will either be amazing or terrible and ignoring all the possibilities in between?	
Do you think that you know what others are thinking about you, and usually assume it's something bad?	
Do you judge yourself negatively for worrying and give yourself a hard time about it?	

If you ticked three or more of these items, you might have picked up some anxious thinking habits. But don't worry, we're going to explore ways you can notice and change these as we continue through this book.

 **Read This** **5 Minutes**

A negative mindset

Humans are hardwired through evolution to jump to negative conclusions to keep themselves safe. Think back to when early people were surviving in the wild. Your life would depend on noticing the dangers around you, from wild animals to dangerous cliffs. Therefore, assuming the worst could help you spot the lion hiding in the bushes and stay alive.

However, having a negative mindset may also mean that you ignore or pay less attention to positive experiences. You may start to fixate on negative events and problems, assume the worst even if things are not really that bad and ignore things that are going well. This worsens anxiety and can make you feel fed up and low.

Some examples of a negative mindset include:

→ constantly being on the lookout for negative comments or criticisms while ignoring all the compliments and nice things that people say

→ worrying obsessively about missing one question on a test, despite achieving a good mark overall and getting praise from your teacher

→ finding it hard to stop thinking about the time you missed a shot or lost a game, even though last week you scored three goals and were voted player of the match

→ assuming you must have done something to annoy your friend when she's quieter than usual, even though she's really upset about an argument with her dad and may not be thinking about you at all

→ constantly comparing yourself negatively with your peers or friendship group.

 **Pause and Think** **5 Minutes**

Can you recognize a negative mindset in the way you look at the world?	

What examples can you think of?	
How does a negative mindset affect your confidence?	
How does it affect your actions and how you live your life? What does it stop you doing? What situations, places or people do you avoid?	

📖 **Read This** 🕐 **5 Minutes**

Anxious thoughts

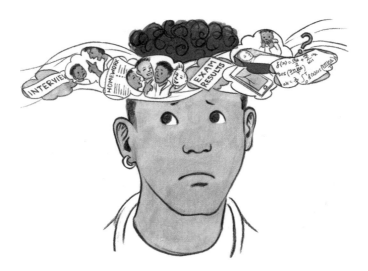

Thoughts involve words and pictures that flow constantly through your mind, helping to make sense of the world around you. Your thoughts can include plans, ideas, hopes, dreams, stories, images, fears and worries, as well as both good and bad memories.

Many thoughts are 'automatic' – they pop into your mind uninvited. And when you have a very sensitive Threat system which is trying to keep you safe from danger, many of these automatic thoughts will focus on difficulties and problems. You might find yourself going over and over your worries and find it hard to think about anything else. Being stuck in anxious thoughts can knock your confidence, distract you from taking helpful action to solve your problems, and often make you feel even more anxious and low.

Some examples of negative thoughts in anxiety include:

→ fears about embarrassing yourself or looking foolish in front of others

→ thinking that anxiety is dangerous or worrying about its effects on your body

→ thinking that you won't be able to cope with problems or with feelings of anxiety

→ focusing on all the dangers in the world or seeing other people as mean and scary

→ remembering times when things have been upsetting and difficult in the past.

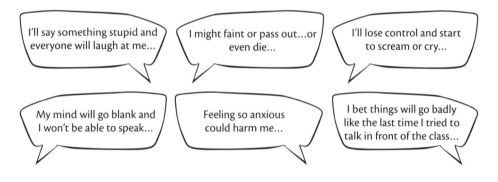

 Pause and Think **5 Minutes**

Do you often find anxious thoughts popping into your mind?	
What are the most common thoughts that show up?	
How do these thoughts make you feel?	
How do these thoughts affect your actions? What do you usually do to prevent them or to get rid of them?	

 **Read This**   **10 Minutes**

Anxious thoughts are common and normal!

If you are struggling with anxiety, you might sometimes feel fed up and frustrated by your anxious thoughts – wondering why your mind never stops thinking about stresses, problems and worries. But it's normal to have lots of thoughts – this is just what our brains do – many of these thoughts will be repeated from the day before.

Having a lot of anxious thoughts just means that your Anxiety Alarm has been switched on and is trying to keep you safe. The problem is not that your mind generates all these negative thoughts. That is how all minds work. It only becomes a problem if you believe everything that your mind is telling you – and if you react as if these anxious thoughts are completely true.

Let's go back to the idea of imagining falling off a cliff. You might picture that in your mind as an anxious thought. But having the thought doesn't mean that it is likely to happen – especially if you stick to a path that's far from the edge. You don't have to 'buy into' or believe the thought or react by not going out for a walk.

Thoughts are not facts

Thoughts often seem especially believable when they come with strong feelings such as anxiety, panic or fear. But even if they *feel* true, your thoughts are often not correct or accurate.

Remember, thoughts are not facts. They are no more than ideas, guesses, possibilities or opinions which pop up in your mind.

You don't have to take your anxious thoughts too seriously or believe everything that your mind tells you, especially about the things that make you anxious. And as we progress through this book, we will cover lots of different skills on how to do this.

 Pause and Think   **5 Minutes**

What's the most important message from this section?	
How can you use this information? What might you do differently as a result?	

Rory says: I have a lot of anxiety thinking habits and a negative mindset. I often find myself thinking about the worst things that can happen, and I forget about all the times that things have gone well. I had a tough time at my last school, and I've lost a lot of confidence, so thinking the worst somehow feels safer, as if I can't be caught out when something goes wrong. But I can also see how thinking about all this bad stuff is making me feel much worse and making it harder to get on in my new college.

It helps to remind myself that I don't have to believe all my negative thoughts when they come. I like the idea that they are just a guess or an opinion – because I often know deep down that I'm thinking the worst and it's not necessarily right.

 **Read This**  **10 Minutes**

Do you get stuck on the Anxiety Train?

Feeling anxious or panicky can be like jumping onto a runaway train. The train goes faster and faster, and each station you pass by is filled with increasingly worrying and terrifying thoughts. As you hurtle down the track, one negative thought leads to another until you are caught up in a whirlwind of anxiety, fear and panic. You feel out of control, and it may seem impossible to get off!

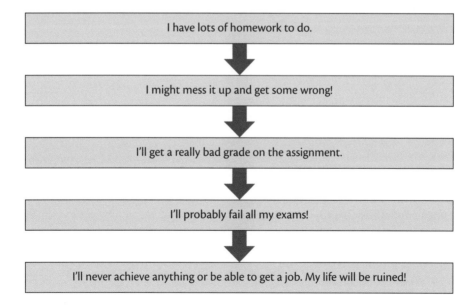

I have lots of homework to do.

I might mess it up and get some wrong!

I'll get a really bad grade on the assignment.

I'll probably fail all my exams!

I'll never achieve anything or be able to get a job. My life will be ruined!

Maya says: My brain is full of anxious thoughts about pretty much everything. I really notice them when I'm not busy – like in the middle of the night or when I'm on my own in my bedroom. Often it starts with something small and then builds up until I'm in a real panic. Then it's like I've jumped straight onto the Anxiety Train, and it is going faster and faster with all my worries there and no way to get away from them.

Passengers on the Anxiety Train

One way to make anxious thoughts feel less distressing is to create a character or an image to go with the most common thoughts that pop up in your mind. This helps you to step back from them and see them as unhelpful thoughts – not believable facts.

Think of your thoughts as outspoken, talkative passengers who jump on the Anxiety Train at each station. They want to tell you about all the scary things that can happen, and they only talk about problems, risks and danger ahead. They have a very negative mindset and will usually:

→ **exaggerate the risks:** they assume the worst will happen and things will be a disaster

→ **focus on what could go wrong:** they only think about possible problems and ignore what could go well

→ **demand your attention:** they make a lot of noise so it's hard to focus on anything else

→ **go round and round:** they don't give up easily and keep going on and on about risks and problems like a broken record

→ **tell you that you can't cope:** so you feel overwhelmed and don't plan how to deal with difficulties.

Pause and Think **5 Minutes**

Here are some of the common passengers on the Anxiety Train. Do you recognize any of these?

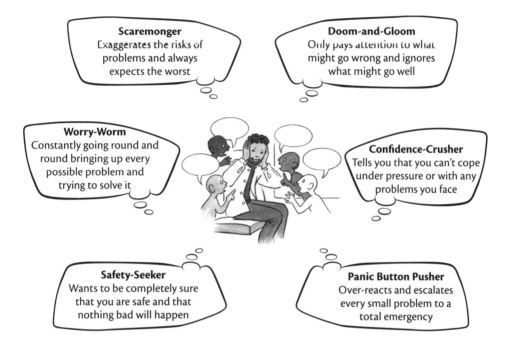

Scaremonger
Exaggerates the risks of problems and always expects the worst

Doom-and-Gloom
Only pays attention to what might go wrong and ignores what might go well

Worry-Worm
Constantly going round and round bringing up every possible problem and trying to solve it

Confidence-Crusher
Tells you that you can't cope under pressure or with any problems you face

Safety-Seeker
Wants to be completely sure that you are safe and that nothing bad will happen

Panic Button Pusher
Over-reacts and escalates every small problem to a total emergency

 Pause and Think **10 Minutes**

Meet your Anxiety Train passengers

Use this table to think about which passengers most often show up in your mind, and how you react when they appear.

Which anxiety passengers most often jump on your train? Do you usually have one or two, or do they show up together as a group?	

Create an image for each passenger. What do they look like? Can you see them as animated characters, animals or funny little creatures? Can you find a way for them to be light-hearted or amusing rather than too serious and scary?	
What do they sound like? What kind of voice would each passenger have? Is it high-pitched and squeaky, loud, hoarse, shouty or an intense whisper? Give different characters a voice that suits them best.	
What kind of things does each passenger say? What do they want to tell you or warn you about? What types of dire predictions or problems do they bring up?	
What do you usually do when the passengers show up? Do you argue with them? Do you believe what they say? Or do you avoid things so that you don't have to hear them going on and on?	
How do these passengers affect your life? What are you missing out on because of the passengers and their negative messages? Do you feel stuck on the train going in a direction you don't like but feeling powerless to change it because of your anxiety?	

Maya says:

Which anxiety passengers most often jump on your train?	*I recognize all these passengers! Worry-Worm is there a lot of the time and never shuts up! Every time I have a test or an exam, Confidence-Crusher shows up and tells me I'm bound to mess it up. And when I get really stressed, it's Panic Button Pusher who starts kicking off.*
Create an image for each passenger.	*I imagine them all like little creatures fighting to get on the train. They might all be a different colour and with differently shaped ears and noses.*
What do they sound like?	*They would be constantly talking the whole time...even in the quiet carriage! Some would have squeaky, annoying voices. I think Panic Button Pusher has a loud booming voice that makes me feel scared and out of control.*

What kind of things does each passenger say?	*They usually tell me that I'm going to look stupid in front of other people or that I'm going to make a mistake that has a really bad outcome.*
What do you usually do when the passengers show up?	*I try hard not to listen to them and I tell them that they are wrong and that things are not so bad – but they often just keep going on until I get anxious. Then I try to avoid whatever situation is making me feel stressed.*
How do these passengers affect your life?	*I feel tense and worried, and I've lost a lot of confidence because of what the passengers are saying. I've stopped going out so much with friends and I feel quite lonely and isolated.*

NAME your Anxiety Train passengers

As we progress through this book, we will explore different ways to cope when the anxiety passengers show up in your mind. For now, can you practise giving each passenger a **NAME**? This is a four-step approach to noticing that the passengers have shown up and that they are trying to tell you what to do.

→ **N**otice that you have started to feel anxious or panicky and how this is affecting your body and emotions. Try saying to yourself 'I'm having some anxious feelings right now. My chest is tight, and my heart is thumping.'

→ **A**cknowledge the Anxiety Train passengers have shown up and greet them by name. Say 'Hi Worry-Worm, hello Scaremonger! I know you both well. Welcome to the train!'

→ **M**ake friends with the passengers – there's no need to fight them, argue with them or try to get rid of them. Just accept that they have shown up and that they have a lot to say, but you don't have to believe every word.

→ **E**xpand your attention. Broaden your focus and notice three things you can see, three things you can hear and three things you can touch around you. This will help you put things in perspective so the passengers are just part of the picture and are no longer bossing you around. Now think about what's most important to do next and do this with as much attention as possible.

Summary: your anxious mind

→ Anxious thoughts are common and normal.

→ Anxious thinking habits can make you more likely to focus on problems and ignore things that are going well.

→ Thoughts are not facts – you don't need to believe everything your mind tells you!

→ Try to see anxious thoughts as imaginary passengers who jump on the Anxiety Train in your mind.

→ Giving anxiety passengers a **NAME** can help you step back and feel less overwhelmed:

> **N**otice how you are feeling.

> **A**cknowledge the passengers who have shown up.

> **M**ake friends with the passengers.

> **E**xpand your attention and do something important.

Final thoughts

Make a note of anything you have found helpful, interesting or surprising from this chapter.

....
....
....
....
....
....

What are you going to do now? Can you choose one small action for the coming week based on what you have read so far?

....
....
....
....
....
....

Chapter 3

ANXIETY AND YOUR ACTIONS

Ruby: I try to avoid things that will make me anxious, but it often catches me out and I can feel suddenly scared or panicky out of the blue. Lately, I can't seem to stop 'doom-scrolling' where I'm constantly searching online for bad news and problems. There's so much bad stuff in the world and reading about it makes me feel so frightened. I wish I could stop but it's like an obsession that I need to keep checking my phone for the latest news.

Waseem: I often don't make it to school because I'm so anxious. I want to go, but thinking about it makes me feel stressed and sick. I was bullied last year and I lost a lot of confidence. The bully has now left the school, but I don't feel I can go back. Instead, I stay at home and play a lot of computer games. I feel better when I'm playing, but afterwards, I feel worse because I know I haven't done anything I wanted to do. Sometimes I feel like a complete failure in life.

 **Read This**  **5 Minutes**

Has anxiety changed how you live your life?

When anxiety gets out of hand, it can have a big impact on how you live your life. Do you miss out on interesting experiences or exciting opportunities because you don't want to trigger your anxiety? Or do you find it hard to concentrate and enjoy things because your mind is caught up with worries about what might go wrong?

It's easy to get stuck in a regular habit of 'anxiety actions', where you constantly plan and organize your life around trying to avoid or reduce anxiety rather than just doing things that make life feel fun and meaningful. In this chapter, we will:

→ explore how anxiety can affect what you do and how you live your life

→ learn how anxiety actions can stop you from doing the things you care about.

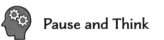 **Pause and Think**  **10 Minutes**

Does anxiety affect your actions?

Complete the following checklist of actions you might take to prevent or cope with feelings of anxiety:

Do you carry out any of these 'anxiety actions' often or very often?	Tick if you have noticed this
Do you avoid situations, people or places that might make you anxious?	
Do you check several times that you've done something correctly?	
Are you spending less time with your friends or getting isolated from your peer group?	
Have you cut down on activities or hobbies because of anxiety?	
Does anxiety make it harder to achieve what you want to at school or work?	
Do you find yourself procrastinating or putting off getting started with important tasks?	
Is it hard to concentrate on activities because of anxiety or worry?	
Do you often ask others for reassurance that you are safe or have done the right thing?	
When you get anxious, do you become clingy and want to stay with someone who feels safe?	
Do you spend ages making lists but never get around to following the steps that you planned?	
Do you try to control or plan every aspect of your life to avoid surprises and feel safer?	
Do you try to distract yourself from anxiety with technology such as computer games or social media?	
Do you react angrily or blame others when you feel anxious?	
Do you try to numb feelings of anxiety with alcohol, food or drugs?	

If you ticked three or more of these answers, then it's likely that anxiety is affecting your actions and your behaviour. As we progress through this book, we will explore many different skills to help you change any unhelpful anxiety actions and react to anxiety in different ways.

Pause and Think **5 Minutes**

How many anxiety actions can you recognize from the list?	
What does this tell you about how much anxiety is affecting your life?	

Waseem says: I ticked about five or six of these answers! I was quite surprised that there were so many ways that anxiety can affect what I do each day. I want to break free and not let anxiety take control of everything I do.

 Read This **10 Minutes**

What is an action?

An action is something that you do or the way you behave in any situation. Most actions can be seen by others – making a drink, studying, going out with friends and going for a walk are all examples of action. Equally, *not* doing these things also involves actions. For example, what are you doing instead of studying? Checking your phone, dozing on the sofa, watching Netflix or playing a computer game are also actions. These may be actions you do to *avoid* doing things that make you feel anxious or distract you from important tasks.

You might also carry out internal actions that take place inside your mind. These can't be seen by other people, but they can still have a big impact on you. Internal actions tend to involve thinking about something repeatedly, such as being caught up in worries or mentally planning for the future.

Most people's actions tend to follow repeated patterns or habits. You might not even notice how often you are carrying them out. But getting stuck with a habit of unhelpful anxiety actions can make you feel even more anxious in the long term, and get in the way of doing other things that may be more important.

Fight Flight Freeze and Find safety

Remember the Fight Flight Freeze reaction when your Anxiety Alarm is set off that we introduced in Chapter 1?

This can also affect your actions. You might have the urge to **Fight** the danger, **Flee** or escape the danger, or you might **Freeze** and feel stuck or overwhelmed. You may also try to **Find** safety by preventing the danger from happening in the first place.

 Pause and Think   **10 Minutes**

Read through the following list and see which anxiety actions you can recognize.

	How might this affect you?	Have you noticed this? What examples can you think of?
Fight	When you start feeling anxious, you might become defensive, irritable or angry and react by getting huffy, snappy or yelling at others.	
Flight or escape	**Leave a situation:** You leave places quickly when you start to feel anxious.	
	Move constantly: You flip from one activity to the next so it's harder to focus and get things finished.	
	Zone out: You escape from anxious feelings by being stuck in your mind and focusing inwards on your thoughts and feelings rather than paying attention to the outside world. Zoning out could also involve using alcohol or drugs to numb or distract you from anxious feelings.	

Freeze or get stuck	**Procrastinate or put off getting started:** You might feel overwhelmed by anxiety and find it difficult to get started on tasks or projects because you feel stuck and unable to take action. You might also become lost for words in a social situation or be unable to think clearly because you are feeling very anxious.	
	Cut down important activities: You might find yourself lacking enthusiasm to do the things you used to enjoy. This will often worsen anxiety as you have more time to spend lost in worry thoughts. This can also lead to you feeling depressed, low and demotivated.	
Find safety	**Avoid what makes you anxious:** You avoid situations, places or people that might make you feel anxious. You stop going to parties, avoid speaking up in a group or class, avoid lifts or busy shops, or you might avoid challenges and choose easier options for fear of failing. You may avoid doing things alone and constantly try to stay with someone who feels safe.	
	Check and double-check: You often find yourself looking for information that makes you feel less anxious. You might find yourself frequently checking health websites or checking your body for symptoms of illness, or you might check repeatedly that you've locked the door or turned the oven off.	
	Ask for reassurance: You often ask other people to reassure you that you are safe or that problems won't happen. This may help at first, but the positive feelings often don't last long and anxiety quickly returns so you need to ask for reassurance again.	

Ruby says: I do a lot of these anxiety actions! Here are some examples from the past few weeks.

Anxiety action	Have you noticed this? What examples can you think of?
Zone out	*When I'm sitting with a group of friends, I focus on my phone and don't get involved in the conversation because I don't want to say something silly.*
Avoid what makes you anxious	*I didn't go to a party I was invited to last weekend because I was worried that I would feel left out and look silly. I stayed home and felt fed up all evening because I knew all my friends were out having fun.*
Check and double-check	*I worry a lot about problems in the world like war or climate change. I often find myself checking news articles to see what's new...hoping to find good news but it's always something bad!*
Ask for reassurance	*I ask my mum a lot when I get anxious, and she always tells me that I shouldn't worry and everything will be fine! I know she's right and it does make me feel better for a while, although the worries often come back later on.*

 Read This 5 Minutes

The effect of anxiety actions

At first glance, many anxiety actions may seem logical and even helpful. They are usually aimed at reducing or preventing uncomfortable feelings of anxiety. So, it makes sense why you may turn to them when anxiety shows up.

But there is a big problem – most of these actions will make anxiety worse in the long run! There are several ways that this can happen:

The more you try to avoid anxiety, the larger it grows! Every time you avoid doing something because of fear or worry, it gives anxiety a super-boost, making it more likely to come back even stronger the next time you face a similar situation. This is because you are not able to discover that the negative thoughts were exaggerated and never likely to happen.

Avoidance makes you lose confidence! When you don't do something because of anxiety, it feels even harder to do next time as you lose confidence in your abilities to deal with problems and challenges.

You miss out on things that matter: Avoiding things that you care about because of anxiety has a negative impact on your life as you miss out on many experiences and opportunities.

The relief doesn't last long! You might feel better at first after asking for reassurance or checking something online, but the relief doesn't usually last long, and you will soon start to feel anxious again.

Anxiety actions are distracting: Carrying out repeated anxiety actions often makes it harder to concentrate or focus and can make your usual activities less enjoyable and satisfying.

 Pause and Think **5 Minutes**

Think back to the examples of your anxiety actions in the table above. Can you notice any unhelpful impact of these actions on your life?

> **Waseem says:** I know that missing school because of anxiety means I'm not getting the chance to learn and study with my teachers. I'm really worried about how it will affect my future chances to go to university and get a job that I like. I also miss seeing my friends at school. Staying at home often feels better at first but I am starting to feel quite isolated and lonely.

 Read This **5 Minutes**

Your actions and the Anxiety Train

Think back to the Anxiety Train that we looked at in Chapter 2. When you get to the train station, you want to take a train going somewhere interesting and exciting. Maybe it will take you towards the career you've always wanted, or perhaps it's a train going somewhere enjoyable. You want to be able to choose for yourself which train to jump on, based on what you are interested in and enjoy.

But sometimes the Anxiety Train passengers show up before you get on the train! Scaremonger and Doom-and-Gloom start telling you how long and dangerous the journey will be. So, you don't get on the train at all, you just hesitate on the platform and then watch the train heading off without you.

Or maybe you are on the train and then Worry-Worm shows up, going on and on about all the problems that might happen when you get off again. It's so distracting that you miss your stop! Now you are stuck on the train feeling lost and unsure where to go next.

Or maybe Panic Button Pusher shows up

and starts yelling about an imminent catastrophe – the train is about to crash! So, you pull the emergency cord, stop the train and then jump straight onto the next train back home again. You feel better at first, but then you realize that you missed out on something important and feel fed up and sad.

 Pause and Think **10 Minutes**

Think back to Chapter 2 and the Anxiety Train passengers who are most likely to show up and affect your life.

Do these passengers affect which train you choose to get on?	
Are they stopping you from being able to enjoy the journey?	
Do they interfere with which train you get on or make you go somewhere that you don't want to be?	

 **Read This** **2 Minutes**

What can you do differently?

The good news is that you don't have to stick with old anxiety habits if they are no longer working. You can choose your actions and can use this to take control of the direction of your life.

Changing your actions involves noticing what you tend to do in anxiety-provoking situations and learning to do something different. This can be a physical action, such as only checking something once, or putting a reminder on your phone to do something important. It can also be a mental action, like noticing which Anxiety Train passenger has shown up, but not responding to it in your usual way. Making tiny changes in your actions can often lead to positive changes as anxiety starts to have less control over how you are living your life.

As you progress through this book, you will learn ways to cope with anxiety in small steps that will gradually build your confidence to do the things you care about.

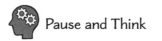 Pause and Think  **10 Minutes**

Can you plan one tiny action that involves changing or cutting down on an anxiety action? What can you do instead? Who can you ask to help with this?

To maximize your chances of success, try to plan something really small that takes less than 5 minutes to complete.

Make a note of what you will try here.

....

....

....

....

....

....

> **Ruby says:** I'm going to cut down on 'doom-scrolling' by 5 minutes in the evening. Instead, I'll watch something fun or light-hearted. I will ask my mum to watch a comedy TV programme with me.
>
> **Waseem says:** I don't feel ready to go back to school, but I'm going to cut down on playing computer games when I'm at home. I'll try to spend 5 minutes doing something for school before starting to play. I could send my teacher an email and ask for some advice about what I can do to keep my grades up at home.

Summary: anxiety and your actions

→ Actions are what you do or how you behave in a situation.

→ Common anxiety actions include avoidance, procrastination, checking, asking for reassurance and zoning out.

→ Repeated anxiety actions give anxiety a 'super-boost' that makes it grow stronger and can make you miss out on enjoyable and exciting experiences and opportunities.

→ You can plan tiny steps to make changes in anxiety actions.

Final thoughts

Make a note of anything you have found helpful, interesting or surprising from this chapter.

....

....

....

....

....

....

What are you going to do now? Can you choose one small action for the coming week based on what you have read so far?

....

....

....

....

....

....

Chapter 4

LOOPS OF ANXIETY

Anushka: I was going home on the bus when two boys sitting in front of me started to argue. One boy leaned forward and got right into the other's face. The argument escalated and they both started yelling. One boy shoved the other and he fell right next to where I was sitting. Then he reached into his pocket, and, for a minute, I thought he was going to pull out a knife.

My heart started pounding and I began to sweat. I felt dizzy and sick. My thoughts were racing. All I could think was that I was going to get hurt in the fight or maybe even stabbed!

Afterwards, whenever I thought about the incident, I started feeling anxious again. My friends seemed able to get past it and after a couple of weeks they didn't mention it again, but I kept on worrying. I couldn't stop thinking how out of control I felt on the bus, and I never wanted to feel that scared again.

I started asking my parents for a lift so I didn't have to take the bus anymore. After a while, I began staying away from crowded areas and shops in case something dangerous happened there too. When I'm in any public place, I constantly look around trying to check if there's any risk of people starting to fight, and if I notice anything like people talking loudly then I ask my parents to take me home.

I'm trying hard to feel safe, but it seems like the more I try to stop feeling anxious, the worse I feel. I'm starting to feel worn out and exhausted with it all.

In the book so far, we have discovered how anxiety affects your body, mind and actions in many different ways. In this next chapter, we will:

→ learn how to use a simple 'Anxiety Map' to make sense of your reactions to anxiety

→ discover how thoughts, feelings, body sensations and actions can link to create loops of anxiety

→ practise creating an Anxiety Map using your own experiences of anxiety.

 Read This   🕐 10 Minutes

Using an Anxiety Map

We can use an Anxiety Map to help you make sense of your reactions when you become anxious. When you have a map of an area then you can understand where you are now, and you will have a better idea of which direction to take in the future!

This involves looking at five different areas of your anxiety reaction.

Area of anxiety	What to ask yourself	What might you notice?
The situation or trigger	What is happening that is causing you to feel anxious?	It might be a situation in the present or something coming up in the future that you are concerned about.
Your feelings and emotions	Which emotions and feelings arise when you are anxious?	You might notice many different feelings such as nervousness, unease, fear and panic.
In your body	What are the physical reactions that occur in your body when your Anxiety Alarm goes off?	There may be many different body reactions including your heart thumping, butterflies in your tummy, feeling shaky or sweating, or fast breathing.
What you think	What thoughts and images appear when you feel anxious?	You may develop anxious thinking habits that trigger many anxious thoughts such as worrying about looking foolish, making a mistake or fears about possible dangers and risks in the world.
Your actions	What actions do you often take to prevent or cope with feelings of anxiety?	You may carry out anxiety actions which involve the automatic Fight Flight Freeze or Find safety responses. These include avoiding or putting off things that make you anxious, checking and double-checking, asking for reassurance and zoning out.

The anxiety passengers change your thinking and you:
• exaggerate the danger
• focus on everything that could go wrong
• keep going over and over the problem
• believe you can't cope so you lose confidence.

There are changes in your body such as: shaking, sweating, muscle tension, rapid breathing, racing heart, feeling sick.

You might feel: fearful, anxious, scared, worried, afraid, panicky or overwhelmed.

You carry out anxiety actions such as:
Fight – get angry or irritable
Flight – leave places that make you anxious
Freeze – put off or cut down activities
Find safety – avoid or put off things that make you anxious, check and double-check, ask for reassurance.

Example of an Anxiety Map

Anushka says: I wasn't sure how to fill in the Anxiety Map at first because all the different parts felt a bit mixed up. But when I thought about it carefully, I could see that each part was happening even if it was very quick.

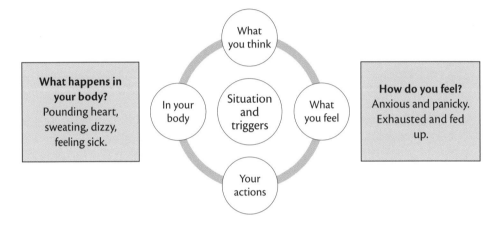

What was the situation or trigger for anxiety?
I was on the bus when two boys had a fight near me. Afterwards, my anxiety was triggered every time I thought about getting on a bus or being in a busy place.

What thoughts come up when you are anxious?
I might get hurt or stabbed.
I keep thinking about the scary incident.
I never want to feel so out of control and scared again.

What happens in your body?
Pounding heart, sweating, dizzy, feeling sick.

What you think

Situation and triggers

In your body

What you feel

Your actions

How do you feel?
Anxious and panicky. Exhausted and fed up.

What anxiety actions can you notice?
I avoid going on buses – I ask my parents to drive me.
I stay away from crowded areas and shops.
I often check for danger in public places.
I go home if people are talking loudly around me.

Anushka's Anxiety Map

 **Do This** **10 Minutes**

Your own Anxiety Map

Now, choose an example of a recent situation when you felt anxious to practise creating an Anxiety Map. Choose a time that you felt just a little anxious or nervous rather than a really scary or overwhelming experience. Fill in each part of the Anxiety Map below.

What was the situation or trigger for anxiety?

What thoughts came up? Which anxiety passengers paid you a visit?

What happened in your body?			How did you feel?

What
you think

In your
body

Situation
and
triggers

What
you feel

Your
actions

What anxiety actions did you notice (e.g.: Fight, Flight, Freeze, Find safety)?

 Pause and Think   10 Minutes

What do you notice when you break down your reaction using an Anxiety Map? Does anything seem different?	
Are there any links between different areas of the map? For example, do negative thoughts, unpleasant feelings or body sensations lead to you taking anxiety actions?	
Does looking at the map suggest anything that might help you to cope better with your anxiety? What is this?	

The main aim of this section of the book is to help you understand more about anxiety and to make sense of what happens when you feel anxious. As we move through the rest of the book, you will learn new skills to deal with anxiety in different ways and use your Anxiety Map to help you move in whatever life direction you want.

Summary: loops of anxiety

→ You can use an Anxiety Map to break down your anxiety into five areas:

> the situation or trigger for anxiety

> your feelings and emotions

> what happens in your body when you get anxious

> what happens in your mind and how you think

> changes in your behaviour such as Anxiety Actions.

→ Using an Anxiety Map can help you understand your reactions and plan your route to move beyond anxiety and towards the life you most want.

Final thoughts
Make a note of anything you have found helpful, interesting or surprising from this chapter.

....

....

....

....

What are you going to do now? Can you choose one small action for the coming week based on what you have read so far?

....

....

....

....

Part 2

DIFFERENT TYPES OF ANXIETY

Chapter 5

STRESSFUL SITUATIONS AND PROBLEMS

Is your anxiety being triggered by particular problems or stressful life situations? Are you struggling with the pressures of schoolwork and exams or wanting to succeed in a particular career? Perhaps you are having problems in relationships with friends or family, or with others on social media.

Life events and circumstances can bring specific challenges. It can be hard to find a balance between fitting in with your peer group, while also finding your identity and interests as an individual. Some circumstances, such as home life or demands at school, may not be within your control. Feeling anxious or panicky can also make it harder to deal with these problems and situations in helpful ways.

In this chapter, we will:

→ learn how to recognize problems that can trigger feelings of anxiety

→ recognize which problems have a practical solution you can do something about

→ explore what mindset makes it easier to cope with problems

→ look at some simple steps to deal with problems effectively.

Chen: I'm feeling so anxious and overwhelmed at the moment. Our mock exams are starting next week, and I don't think I've prepared enough, but I'm struggling to concentrate on studying because I get so stressed and anxious. Things are difficult at home at the moment because I'm not getting on well with my stepdad and there are lots of arguments and constant stress. I get worked up and I keep having disagreements with my girlfriend about silly things. I keep thinking that she might break up with me. It all feels like too much to deal with right now.

What problems are triggering your anxiety?

Many different situations and problems can lead to feelings of anxiety, especially if you are feeling powerless or unsure of what steps to take that may help. Making a list of the problems that you are dealing with can help you feel less out of control and make things feel easier to manage.

Look at this list of different types of problems. Make a note of any that you are dealing with at the moment.

Different types of problem	Is this a problem for you?	What's happening? How is it affecting you?
Living up to pressures or expectations for your behaviour or your performance at school or in other areas of life		
Difficulties with friendships and peer groups, including bullying		
Keeping up with extracurricular activities or sports		
Coping with change, such as moving house, leaving school, starting work or university		
Managing your time – feeling overloaded with things to do, unprepared or overwhelmed		
Disagreements, difficulties or conflict at home or with family relationships		

Problems with a partner, girlfriend or boyfriend		
Money worries or not having the funds to do what you want		
What other problems are you dealing with? Write them down here:		

How do you react to problems?

How do you react when you are facing a problem, difficult situation or complicated decision? You might experience many different emotions such as feeling anxious, tense, stressed, angry, frustrated, confused and overwhelmed, or you may feel excited and enthusiastic. In your body, you may feel tired, heavy, achy, sick or become agitated and need to move around.

When you are feeling anxious about a problem, the Anxiety Train passengers may show up in your mind, exaggerating the risks and focusing on the worst possible things that may happen. You might hear them saying things like:

This is going to be a disaster!

You can never cope with this!

Everyone will think badly of you!

If you listen to these anxious thoughts, you are likely to feel even more stressed and worried. You might find yourself taking unhelpful actions such as avoiding facing up to problems or panicking and making rash decisions that you will later regret.

There is no need to argue with the Anxiety Train passengers when they show up, but you don't have to believe everything they say. You can start to see problems as an opportunity to find solutions and learn about yourself and the world. As you start to believe that you can cope with any problems that life throws at you, your confidence will grow and your anxiety may become less of a problem.

 Pause and Think **10 Minutes**

A problem-solving mindset

How you approach problems will have a big impact on how you feel and how well you can cope with difficult situations. Look at our tips for building a problem-solving mindset. Which of these can you use next time you are facing a problem?

Tips for a problem-solving mindset	How could you use this tip? What can you do differently?
Pinpoint the problem: when you first notice a sense of unease or anxiety, pause and investigate. What exactly is the problem? You may find the NAME exercise on page 63 helpful here. Pausing, stepping back and identifying the problem is the first step to resolving it.	
See problems as challenges: think of it as a puzzle that takes a little time and effort, rather than a major threat or a catastrophe. This will help you take positive action rather than trying to avoid or put off dealing with the issue.	
Focus on what you can control: the more you focus on things you cannot influence or change, the more anxious you may feel. What parts of the situation do you have some control over? It's easier to take charge of your actions than to control your thoughts or feelings, or how other people behave or react.	
Start small and build up: don't try to solve your most difficult problems all at once. Build your confidence by making small changes and notice what effect this has.	

Remember your strengths: what personal skills, strengths and abilities can you call on to help you deal with this problem?	
Talk to someone you trust: don't go it alone when facing problems! Who can you turn to for advice, support or encouragement?	

Take positive action about problems

You will often start to feel better as you begin to take constructive action about solving problems. Sometimes the solution is quite straightforward and obvious – it's clear what you need to do to fix the problem, and you have the skills to do it. At other times, the answer may be less clear and you may need to try out several options before you find the best solution.

And remember – you can't 'fix' everything, nor can you do it all at once! You may need to break things down into small steps and take one at a time, and you may not get a 'perfect' result. But taking more positive action can build your confidence as you feel more in control of the situation and more able to deal with challenges and make decisions.

 **Pause and Think** **10 Minutes**

Steps for solving problems

There is a simple step-by-step approach to solving practical problems, which can also help with making complicated decisions and difficult choices.

Step 1: Name the problem

The first step is to choose a problem to focus on first. It's usually helpful to begin by choosing problems that are small as these may be easier to solve. Also, try to pick problems that you have some control over and where you have the power to change at least part of the situation.

Be specific about what you are concerned about, for example:

➜ You really want to buy a new pair of trainers, but you don't have the money.

➜ You keep arguing with your sister because she constantly makes a mess in your shared bedroom.

➜ You have an important test coming up, but you've also been invited to a party and you don't know what do to.

➜ Your friend said something mean about you behind your back and you are worried about what everyone thinks about you.

Make a note of your problem here:

My problem is that...

....

....

....

Chen says: I don't know how to plan my study time. I'm feeling overwhelmed by all the work I need to do for my mock exams. I keep thinking that I'm going to fail completely and that the real exams next year will be even worse. My stepdad complains that I am not working hard enough, and we argue, which makes me more stressed.

Step 2: What's important?

The next step is to think about why this problem matters to you and what is most important. Answer the following questions.

Why does this matter to you? Why is it important?	
What are your biggest fears or worries about this?	
What would you like to happen? What would be the best outcome?	

Chen says:

Why does this matter to you? Why is it important?	*It's important to get good grades in my exams so I can have choices about going to university and a job that I like.*
What are your biggest fears or worries about this?	*I get panicky that I'm going to fail completely and that my life will be totally ruined. I'm more irritable and it makes me argue more.*
What would you like to happen? What would be the best outcome?	*I would like to pass with a good grade but also to feel less stressed and worried about it, so I can enjoy life more and not end up arguing with my stepdad or losing my girlfriend!*

Step 3: Brainstorm ideas for solutions

Next, it's time to make a list of all the possible ways that you could solve the problem. Let your imagination run wild and write down everything that comes to mind, even if some of the ideas are unlikely or impractical. Try to use your sense of humour, as this can help you to be creative in how you approach the problem and may help you to find a wider range of possible solutions.

My list of solutions to the problem:

....

....

....

....

....

Chen says: Here is a list of all the solutions I could think of. I could:

➜ study every day as hard as I can after school and really push myself to concentrate more

➜ give up completely and not bother to study at all

➜ set a timer and try to study for a short time every day

➜ study with my friend to make it more fun

➜ go for a walk or a jog before I study to try and calm myself down and get more focused

➜ ask my teacher for some tips on how to study.

Step 4: Compare the solutions

Think about each solution and how good you think it is – will it solve the problem completely or maybe even just a little? Think about what is 'for' and 'against' each suggestion. You can cross off any solutions that you know won't work or won't be helpful.

If you are struggling to come up with ideas, you could try talking through the different possibilities with someone that you trust to get some more suggestions.

Possible solution	What's 'for' this solution? How could it help?	What's 'against' this solution? Are there any problems with it?

Here are Chen's answers.

Possible solution	What's 'for' this solution? How could it help?	What's 'against' this solution? Are there any problems with it?
Study every day as hard as I can and push myself to concentrate more.	I might get more studying done.	I'm not sure if this would work and I might get very anxious or tired.
Give up completely and not bother to study at all.	It would take away the pressure and I would have time for other things.	I don't want to fail the test, and this might make me feel worse.
Set a timer and try to study for a short time every day.	This might be less stressful as I would be doing some studying but not too much.	What if I don't get enough done?

Study with my friend to make it more fun.	*This would definitely be more fun, and he might have some ideas about what to learn.*	*We could end up chatting and not getting much work done.*
Go for a walk or a jog before I study to try and calm myself down and get more focused.	*I usually focus much better after I exercise, so this might help. It also makes me feel calmer and more relaxed.*	*I might not feel like going out if I'm tired after school.*
Ask my teacher for some tips on how to study.	*This could give me some ideas or websites to use that can help me to study more effectively.*	*She might not be very helpful, or I might not find her ideas useful.*

Step 5: Pick a solution to try

Now it's time to choose one or more solutions to try. Pick the one that seems most practical, helpful and has the best chance of success. It doesn't have to completely fix the problem! Most of the time solutions are not perfect – they're just OK. If there are several choices, you might be able to use more than one solution.

What solution(s) will you try out first?	
Do you need any more information to help you choose or to carry it out successfully? How and where can you find this out?	

Chen says:

What solution(s) will you try out first?	I'd like to try out jogging before studying to see if it helps me concentrate, and maybe also just try to study for a shorter time.
Do you need any more information to help you choose or to carry it out successfully? How or where can you find this out?	I will talk to my teacher about what is the most important subject to focus on first.

Step 6: Put it into practice

The next step is to try out your chosen solution. You might need to break this down into small steps to make it easier to carry it out. You can keep other options as backup plans in case things don't work out with your first solution.

What am I going to do?	
When and where will I do it?	
Can I make this solution any smaller or easier to carry out?	
Can I get any help with doing it?	

Chen says:

What am I going to do?	I will go for a 15-minute jog after school before I start studying and then set a timer for an hour of revision.
When and where will I do it?	I will go for a jog around our local park on Monday after school at 4 pm.
Can I make this solution any smaller or easier to carry out?	I could set the timer for a shorter time – maybe half an hour of studying.
Can I get any help with doing it?	My mum might go with me if I don't feel like going out.

Step 7: Well done! What happened?

After you try the solution, stop and congratulate yourself! Remember, it's great to take action and get some practice at solving problems no matter what happens. How do you feel now?

It's also time to think about what you tried to do and what happened. Did it solve the problem, or do you need to try something else? Sometimes it takes time for a solution to make things better, and not every solution will be helpful. Part of effective problem-solving is being able to adapt and change if things don't go as planned. If necessary, you can return to Step 1 and try again. Perhaps the problem wasn't what you thought it was, or the solutions weren't quite right.

Ask yourself the following questions.

What went well? What was helpful?	
What didn't go so well?	
What could make this solution easier or more effective?	
What am I going to do next?	

Chen says:

What went well? What was helpful?	*I set the timer for half an hour of studying and managed to get quite a lot done.*
What didn't go so well?	*I couldn't go for a jog because I had a sore knee from playing rugby.*
What could make this solution easier or more effective?	*I could try going for a walk instead of a run.*
What am I going to do next?	*Tomorrow I will go for a 10-minute walk and then study for half an hour again. If it all goes to plan, I might arrange a coffee with my girlfriend at the weekend as a reward!*

 Do This    **10 Minutes**

The problem-solving steps

Here is a reminder of all the steps for problem-solving. You can use this to think about any problem or difficult situation that you are facing.

Step 1	**Name the problem:** Choose a small problem where you can make some changes in the situation.	
Step 2	**What's important?** Why does this matter to you? What would you like to happen?	
Step 3	**Brainstorm solutions:** Make a list of all the ideas you can think of.	
Step 4	**Compare the solutions:** Think about what is 'for' and 'against' each option and which one seems most helpful.	
Step 5	**Pick a solution to try:** Choose one or more ideas to try out. Do you need any more information or advice?	

Step 6	**Put it into practice:** Make a plan of what you will do and where and when to try it. Can you make it easier or get help with carrying it out?	
Step 7	**Well done! What happened?** Congratulate yourself for trying problem-solving and then think about what went well. What was helpful? What didn't go so well? What will you do next?	

What if you can't fix the problem?

Sometimes, it may not be possible to completely solve a big or complicated problem, but just taking small steps towards solving one part of it may help you feel more in control and reduce your anxiety. You may need to find ways to live with some unease, discomfort or uncertainty. Talking it through and getting support will help with this.

You may also need to find ways to accept some things you cannot change, such as past events, other people's reactions or feelings or situations that are a long way in the future. You might also find it helpful to find ways to manage any strong emotions that show up when you are facing problems. We will talk about this more as the book continues.

Summary: stressful situations and problems

→ Taking positive action to deal with problems can help to overcome your anxiety as you feel more in control and able to deal with the issues you are facing.

→ The steps for solving practical problems are:

> Name the problem

> What's important

> Brainstorm ideas for solutions

> Compare the solutions

> Pick a solution to try

> Put it into practice

> Well done! What happened?

Final thoughts

Make a note of anything you have found helpful, interesting or surprising from this chapter.

....

....

....

....

....

....

What are you going to do now? Can you choose one small action for the coming week based on what you have read so far?

....

....

....

....

....

....

Chapter 6

PANIC ATTACKS

Panic attacks are intense feelings of fear and anxiety. Not everyone with anxiety will be affected by panic attacks, but if you do experience one, it can be extremely unpleasant and scary.

Panic attacks usually come on suddenly and can feel overwhelming. There are often strong body sensations, such as a racing heart or a tight chest, which can feel extremely unpleasant and frightening. You can feel out of control or disconnected from what's happening around you. You might feel terrified that something really bad is happening to you and it may seem like you are in danger.

It's important to remember that although panic attacks are scary and uncomfortable, they are not dangerous and the feelings will always pass in a short time. In this chapter, we will start to make sense of panic attacks as we:

➜ discover what happens in your body and mind during a panic attack

➜ learn a simple tool for reducing feelings of panic.

Poppy: I walked into my form room and my heart started beating so hard it felt like it was about to jump right out of my chest. Suddenly, completely out of nowhere, the lights seemed way too bright, the world went out of focus and I felt sick. I felt like I was suffocating and I even thought I might be dying. I felt dizzy and faint and I'm sure everyone was staring at me. I just managed to run to the toilet, feeling like I was going to collapse at any moment. I sat for ages in tears, feeling embarrassed and humiliated. Afterwards, I didn't want to go back into registration in case it happened again.

Pause and Think **10 Minutes**

What is a panic attack?

Panic attacks come on quickly, usually over a few minutes, and can be unexpected. However, they usually only last about 20–40 minutes, so they will also pass very quickly.

Look at the following checklist to see if you can recognize some feelings or body sensations that can happen during a panic attack.

What happens during a panic attack	Do you recognize this? What examples can you think of?
Strong feelings of fear, anxiety or terror	
Heart racing or thumping in your chest	
Sweating, shaking or trembling	
Numbness or tingling	
Difficulty breathing	
Feeling that you are choking	
Chest pain or discomfort	
Feeling sick or having tummy pain	
Feeling detached or that things are not real around you	
Being scared that you might pass out or faint	
Fear of losing control or going crazy	
Fear of being seriously ill or even dying	

If you have ticked yes to three of more of these questions, then it may be time to work on your feelings of anxiety and panic.

Understanding panic

One of the best ways to understand what happens during a panic attack is to use an Anxiety Map to explore what happens in your body and mind.

Situations and triggers for panic attacks

Panic attacks can happen anywhere and at any time, even during the night. You might have a specific trigger, for example, a particular place, or there may be no clear reason and a panic attack can just come 'out of nowhere'.

You may be more likely to experience a panic attack if you are feeling very anxious about difficult situations in your life, such as some of the different problems and life stresses we discussed in Chapter 5.

 Pause and Think **10 Minutes**

What situations or places might trigger a panic attack?

Make a note of any situations where you have experienced high levels of anxiety or a panic attack, including:

→ specific places that make you feel panicky such as busy shops or classrooms

→ situations that cause a lot of anxiety, such as having to speak in front of others, or going places alone

→ thoughts or memories of distressing events and experiences that trigger feelings of panic.

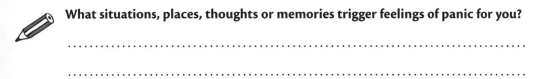

What situations, places, thoughts or memories trigger feelings of panic for you?

....

....

....

....

Body changes in panic

There can be many sudden and intense changes in your body during a panic attack. This is because your body's Anxiety Alarm system has been set off, and it often has a really loud siren to alert you to possible danger.

You will remember from Chapter 1 that this triggers the Fight Flight Freeze reaction, which leads to many different physical feelings and sensations as your body prepares to fight, run away or hide from a threatening situation. During a panic attack, these symptoms escalate and can become extreme.

 Pause and Think **10 Minutes**

How does your body react during a panic attack?

Look at the list below which shows what can happen to your body during a panic attack. Make a note of any sensations that you have noticed.

What happens to your body	What you might notice	Have you noticed this? What happens in your body?
Your heart beats faster to pump blood to the muscles so they are ready to fight or run.	A thumping or racing heart which beats strongly in your chest.	
You breathe faster and deeper to deliver more oxygen around the body.	This can cause discomfort and tightness in the muscles of your chest. Because you are breathing so deeply, it might feel like it's hard to catch your breath. Rapid breathing also leads to 'hyperventilation', which makes you feel dizzy or light-headed and causes tingling in your hands and around your mouth. However, because of your rapid heartbeat, you are unlikely to faint or pass out during a panic attack.	

Increased sweating to cool your body.	You might feel hot and sweaty.	
You have a dry mouth and swallow frequently.	You might find it harder to swallow because of reduced saliva, which can cause tension and discomfort, or a feeling like there is a lump in your neck and throat.	
The body shifts blood away from your gut and digestion to your muscles.	You might feel sick, have a churning stomach or tummy cramps, or need to go to the toilet.	
Your muscles tense up and prepare to fight or run.	Tension in your muscles can make you feel shaky or have wobbly legs. This can also cause headaches and back and neck discomfort and you may feel tired and heavy afterwards.	
Your pupils dilate to allow more light in and help you see danger more easily.	You might notice blurred vision, spots in front of your eyes, or the light may seem very bright.	
You become very alert with sharpened senses that focus only on the possible danger.	You may become jumpy and sensitive to sounds, become forgetful or find it hard to concentrate on other things.	
In the freeze response, your body stays completely still, trying to hide from a predator.	You might feel stuck as if you can't move. You might feel like you are detached or disconnected from your body.	

As you can see from this list, there are a great many different body sensations that can occur during anxiety or a panic attack. The most important thing to remember is that these body changes may be unpleasant and scary, but *they are not dangerous and will not harm you*. Keeping this in mind can help to prevent anxiety from spiralling upwards into a panic attack.

> **Poppy says:** I have lots of these body changes! I was surprised to find out how many things I might feel in my body when I'm very anxious. It helped me to find out that these changes are just part of the Anxiety Alarm system and that they are not dangerous or harmful. Next time I feel panicky, I'll try and remind myself that I'm not in danger and the feelings in my body will go away after a short time.

 Pause and Think **10 Minutes**

Feelings and emotions

During a panic attack, you will usually start feeling very anxious and this can escalate very quickly to become terror and panic.

What emotions can you notice during a panic attack? How long do they usually last?

....

....

....

Remember, these feelings will usually only last for around 20 minutes. Spotting the signs and knowing that it is anxiety – unpleasant but not dangerous – can help.

 **Read This** **10 Minutes**

Thoughts during a panic attack

During a panic attack, it's common to have lots of anxious and panicky thoughts. You may notice that many Anxiety Train passengers show up in your mind, especially Panic Button Pusher!

They will exaggerate the danger that you are facing and insist that you are not able to cope with it. They might tell you that the body sensations you are having are dangerous and harmful, rather than normal reactions to anxiety. Or they might focus on how you appear to others, saying you look foolish or that others will think badly of you.

You might have thoughts such as:

This feels really bad! I am in danger!

I can't breathe! I'm choking!

Maybe I'm having a heart attack!

I can't cope with feeling like this!

I'm going to faint! I might even die!

Everyone is looking at me and laughing!

These thoughts lead to an increase in feelings of anxiety which can rapidly build up to a panic attack. We will explore more about how to cope with anxious thoughts in Chapter 14. For now, your goal is to start to notice what type of thoughts you have when you become anxious or panicky.

 **Pause and Think** 🕐 **10 Minutes**

Your anxious thoughts
When you become panicky, what kinds of thoughts do you have?

....
....
....

Which Anxiety Train passengers show up? Does Panic Button Pusher pay you a visit?

....
....
....

What effect do these thoughts have on your feelings of anxiety?

....

....

....

 Pause and Think 10 Minutes

Your actions

When you feel panicky, you will often act in some way either to prevent the problem or to escape from a scary situation. As we learned in Chapter 3, this means that you will often choose actions that involve Fight Flight Freeze or Finding safety.

Look at the list of panicky actions below. Which of these can you recognize?

Panicky action	Do you recognize this? What actions do you usually take?
Fight: You may get defensive, angry or start yelling at others.	
Flight or escape: You leave the situation as quickly as possible. You may also avoid going to places or situations that could trigger panicky feelings.	
Freeze or get stuck: You might find yourself staying very still, unable to move, think clearly or talk.	
Find safety: You do things to try and prevent a panic attack. You might try to distract yourself, carry objects or stay near people that make you feel safer.	

It may seem like panicky actions are helping but they can also cause problems. Avoiding things that make you anxious can restrict your life and stop you from doing things that are enjoyable or important to you. This will also make you lose confidence and can increase your anxiety in the long term. We will explore how to choose more helpful actions for overcoming anxiety and panic attacks in Chapter 12: Ready for Action.

Poppy says: I usually try to 'escape' from panicky situations. As soon as I start feeling anxious in a class, I leave straight away. That makes me feel less anxious but I'm missing a lot of classes and it feels embarrassing to go back in afterwards. I've also been avoiding going to the canteen at lunchtime because it is so busy and I'm scared I might have a panic attack in front of so many people. That means I miss having lunch with my friends. I often have to sit by myself and eat my sandwich outside. I'm starting to feel quite left out.

Tips for coping with panic

Here are our tips to help you overcome panic and reclaim your life.

Remember – it won't last forever! Panic attacks are scary and uncomfortable, and the feeling of anxiety can be very strong, but they will always pass after a short time. Think of panic as a wave to surf on, which will seem very powerful and big for a while, but will rapidly reduce and pass on into the distance.

Write down some helpful advice. It can help to plan in advance what to tell yourself if you are starting to feel anxious or panicky. Write down some helpful reminders such as the following:

→ This is just anxiety and it won't harm me.

→ The feelings are uncomfortable but they won't last long.

→ It will get better soon.

→ I can stay in the situation without needing to run away or avoid it.

→ I have never fainted or had a heart attack!

Talk about it. It can help to talk to someone you trust about how you are feeling. This could be a trusted adult or your doctor or practice nurse. Talking about how you are feeling will help you to make sense of it and get support to ease anxiety and panic.

 **Do This**  **3–5 Minutes**

Beat panic with 54321

Panic attacks can make you feel overwhelmed and out of touch with things around you. A useful skill for dealing with a panic attack is to reconnect with your surroundings using your five senses and noticing what you can see, feel, hear, taste and smell. You can tell yourself 'panic will pass…I am not in danger'. This can help you to step away from anxious thoughts and feelings and feel better able to cope with the situation. Count down panic and turn off your Anxiety Alarm with 54321.

5. Notice five things around you that you can see. What colour are they? *I can see a blue book, a green pen, a yellow pencil, a red coat and a black computer.*

4. Notice four things you can touch with your hands or another part of your body. If it helps, you can try moving your body to create stronger sensations. Describe the texture or feeling. *I can feel my feet on the hard ground, I can feel my toes wriggling, I can feel my hands on the smooth, cool table and by reaching up I can feel my arms stretching.*

3. Take three slow sighing breaths. Breathe in and make your out-breath as long and slow as you can while making a soft sighing sound, 'Haaaaa', or try a gentle long hum. This will help you to breathe with your diaphragm so that your chest muscles feel less tight and uncomfortable. Can you count to five, eight or ten, or higher, as you breathe out? *I can slowly breathe out and count up to 8.*

2. Notice two sounds you can hear in the background. Can you name the loudest and the quietest sounds? *I can hear the hum of traffic and people talking in the next room.*

1. Notice one thing you can smell or taste. You could smell perfume or take a sip of your drink. *I can smell my lip-balm, it smells of cherries, I can take a sip of cool water from my water bottle. Panic will pass…I am not in danger.*

What's next? Remember that you are safe and move on to continue with your day. What's the most important thing you can do right now? Don't allow anxiety or a panic attack to stop you from doing things that you care about. Try to do this activity with as much attention and focus as possible.

If anxiety or panic returns, you can go back through the 54321 steps as many times as you need to.

> **Poppy says:** I was in an English class, and I started feeling anxious. Usually, I would leave straight away, but I decided to try 54321. It wasn't easy to concentrate on it at first, and I didn't think it would help, but I kept trying and went through all of the steps twice. When it came to the second time, I was feeling a lot calmer. I decided that what was most important was to stay in the class and try to focus on learning as best I could, especially because it's a subject I enjoy. I managed to stay for the whole lesson and I felt proud of myself.

Summary: panic attacks

→ Panic attacks are sudden and intense feelings of fear and anxiety.

→ There may be strong body sensations such as a tight chest or a racing heart, which can feel frightening and unpleasant.

→ You may have scary thoughts that you are in danger.

→ Panic attacks are not dangerous and will always pass with time.

→ You can use 54321 to help you cope with panicky feelings and then focus on 'What's next?' to help you get on with what's important.

Final thoughts

Make a note of anything you have found helpful, interesting or surprising from this chapter:

....

....

....

....

....

....

What are you going to do now? Can you choose one small action for the coming week based on what you have read so far?

....

....

....

....

....

....

Chapter 7

WORRY

Everyone worries from time to time. When you face new situations or challenges in life, it's natural to experience some anxiety and worry about whether things will go well and how you will cope with any problems that might get in the way.

But if worry starts to feel out of control, or you are spending a lot of time worrying, then it can start to have a negative effect on your life. Being stuck in your thoughts, constantly thinking about problems or things that could go wrong, rather than focusing on your strengths or achievements, can make you feel anxious and edgy, and undermine your confidence.

In this chapter, we will:

➜ discover what worry is and how it affects your thoughts, emotions, body and actions

➜ learn two simple skills for dealing with worry.

Arjun: It feels like I worry about everything. If I have a test at college, I can't sleep the night before because of worrying that I might mess it up. I also worry a lot about my future and whether I'll be able to make it in the career I want as a pilot. I even worry about things completely out of my control like the future of the planet with global warming or wars happening in the world. Things have been a lot worse over the last year since my grandfather got ill and moved in with us. I keep worrying that he will get worse or that he might die. Seeing him so unwell also makes me worry about my parents' health. If they get even a small cold, I get anxious that they might become seriously unwell too.

 **Read This** **10 Minutes**

Are you stuck on the Worry Roundabout?

Worrying involves thinking about the future in ways that make you feel anxious or fearful. You might find yourself constantly questioning or doubting yourself, or trying to feel completely certain by looking for information and answers to things you feel unsure about. This can become a never-ending cycle of worry. You have got stuck on the Worry Roundabout!

Worry is a human survival skill that allows us to think ahead and plan how to cope with possible danger before it happens. We can problem-solve, keep safe and prevent things from going wrong. However, not all problems can be solved by thinking them through, especially events that are in the future. Therefore, you may become stuck endlessly thinking about the same problems over and over again, which can leave you feeling even more stressed, fearful and fed up.

Everyone worries sometimes about difficult or stressful situations, events or challenges in life. But if worry is taking up a lot of your time or energy, or if constant worry is making you anxious and low, then it may be time to work on your worry habit.

 Pause and Think **10 Minutes**

An Anxiety Map of worry

You can use an Anxiety Map to explore what happens in your body and mind when you worry. Here's a reminder of the different parts of an Anxiety Map.

What do you worry about?

Worry can be caused by any type of problem, such as your health, school or sports performance, family problems, money, safety or world events. Any of these problems can lead to anxiety and worry. It's also possible for worry to be triggered by small problems or

little niggles. Worry thoughts may also seem to pop into your head 'out of the blue', or for no obvious reason.

Use the following chart to make a note of all the things that you tend to worry about.

Triggers for worry	Do you recognize this? What do you tend to worry about?
Do you worry about things that may go wrong in the future?	
Do you worry about your performance at school or work?	
Do you worry about your achievements in assignments or tests, or that you won't reach the goals you have set for yourself?	
Do you have worries about how well you perform in specific activities such as sports, drama, presentations or music?	
Do you worry about friendships, being able to fit in or being accepted socially by others?	
Do you become anxious or preoccupied by world events such as global warming or war?	
Do you worry about your health or safety, or that of your family?	
Do you often worry about something that you said or did in the past?	

If you have ticked yes to three or more of these questions then it may be time to work on your worry!

Pause and Think **10 Minutes**

Feelings and emotions

When you worry, you may feel apprehensive and fearful, and find it harder to relax. You might have feelings of free-floating anxiety or dread that something awful might happen at any moment. Constant worry can also make you feel irritable and tense, and you might start snapping or lashing out at other people. You might also feel fed up, guilty or ashamed about the problems that you are dealing with.

What feelings or emotions do you notice when you worry?

....
....
....

 Pause and Think **10 Minutes**

In the body

Spending a lot of time worrying will make you feel anxious and can cause many of the body sensations that we learned about in Chapter 1. You might notice that your heart beats faster and that you feel tense and sweaty, or find it hard to relax and sit still. You might start pacing around or develop headaches, tummy aches or muscle tension due to constant worry. Worry can also affect your sleep, making it harder to drop off, or you might wake up in the night with a racing mind.

How does worry affect you physically? What can you notice in your body?

....
....
....

 Pause and Think **10 Minutes**

Worry thoughts

Worry involves being trapped in repeated thoughts about possible problems and bad things that may never actually happen. Instead of making you feel better, worrying usually makes you feel worse as problems usually seem to grow bigger and scarier the more you think about them. This makes it hard to stop worrying. When you are stuck on the Worry Roundabout, it's often hard to get off again.

When you worry, it's common to have 'What if...?' thoughts such as:

What are the 'What if...?' questions you often ask yourself? Make a note of the most common worry thoughts you notice.

....

....

....

We will learn skills for coping with 'What if...?' thinking in Chapter 14.

 Pause and Think **10 Minutes**

Worry actions

When you worry a lot, it's common to try and make yourself feel better by choosing worry actions. Unfortunately, most of these actions keep you feeling anxious and stuck and can make your worries escalate. Look at this list of worry actions and make a note of any that you recognize.

Worry action	Do you recognize this? What do you tend to do when you are worried?
Do you frequently ask for reassurance from others that you are safe or that things will turn out OK?	

cont.

Worry action	Do you recognize this? What do you tend to do when you are worried?
Do you tend to put off making decisions or starting activities that might make you anxious or worried?	
Do you try to avoid situations such as going to new or unfamiliar places that might trigger your worry?	
Does worry ever stop you from doing things that are important or that you care about?	
Do you push yourself hard and over-prepare for tests or performances due to worrying that it won't be 'perfect'?	
Do you get distracted by worry so it's hard to enjoy what you are doing?	
Do you find yourself checking or carrying out specific actions to reduce or control worry thoughts?	

Arjun: Using the Anxiety Map was really helpful to make sense of what happens when I worry. I noticed:

Feelings: I often feel anxious and stressed.

In my body: I feel tense in my shoulders, arms and legs, and sometimes I can get shaky. My heart thumps and I feel hot and sick. I often get worried at night, and then it's hard to get to sleep so I feel tired in the morning.

Worry thoughts: I have a lot of 'what if...?' thoughts where I constantly think about things I might have done wrong at school or imagine myself looking foolish in front of the other students. I worry a lot about making the wrong decision or choosing the wrong thing, even for something small or silly. It makes decisions and finding solutions hard.

Worry actions: I often ask my parents for reassurance, and I push myself hard to try to make sure that nothing will ever go wrong. It's really hard work and sometimes I feel exhausted.

 Do This 5 Minutes

Working through worry

We will learn lots of ways to stop worrying as we continue through this book. For now, we will focus on two quick skills you can use to stop worry from escalating and taking over your life.

Notice the NOW for worry

The first step involves using the skill Notice the NOW that we learned about in Chapter 1. There are three steps.

Notice and name your worries using the Anxiety Map as a framework.	*Thoughts: I'm worrying about what I said at school today. I'm having lots of 'What if...?' thoughts about the test tomorrow.* *Feelings: I'm feeling anxious and tense.* *In your body: My heart is thumping and I feel hot and sick.* *Actions: I want to be alone in my room. I want to keep thinking about this over and over again.*
Observe your body and the world around you: Use this to step off the Worry Roundabout and get unstuck from your worry thoughts. Use your five senses to notice what you can see, hear, touch, taste and smell.	*I can see a red pen and a blue book. I can hear the rain outside the window. I can feel a cold glass of water in my hands and take a slow sip.*
What's important? What's next? Take a few minutes to do something enjoyable, important or meaningful with as much attention as possible. Don't let worry get in the way of living your life!	*I can come out of my bedroom and chat with my sister. I can go out for a walk. I can get started with the homework I've been putting off due to worry.*

Put worry 'on hold' with 'Thinking Time'

Thinking Time is a way of cutting down on how much time you spend worrying. Instead of worrying constantly throughout the day, you can plan a regular time to think through any worries or problems you are facing.

If worries pop into your mind at other times, you can choose to put off worrying or put it 'on hold' until your planned Thinking Time.

 Do This  **10 Minutes**

Plan your Thinking Time

Use these steps to plan your daily Thinking Time.

Step 1: Plan your Thinking Time	Choose 15–30 minutes for Thinking Time each day, ideally at the same time and in the same place, and not just before bedtime.
Step 2: Put the worry 'on hold'	If a worry pops into your mind at another time of day, tell yourself: *It's OK to have this worry, but I will deal with it later. I'm going to put off thinking about it until Thinking Time.* You can make a note of any worries or problems you want to remember in a journal or on your phone. After writing it down, close the book again until Thinking Time.
Step 3: Focus on your daily life	After noting down your worry, close the book and focus your attention back on whatever activity you are carrying out. This will help to let go of the worry until Thinking Time later on. Don't be concerned if the same thought pops back again very quickly. Just repeat the same process: accept the thought, write it down and put it on hold for later.
Step 4: It's Thinking Time	Now it's time to think about these problems as much as you like! You might find it helpful to write down your thoughts in a journal or notebook. Look through your list of worries or problems. Cross anything off the list that is no longer a concern. Try to use the problem-solving skills from Chapter 5 to help you cope with any practical problems. Continue Thinking Time for no more than 30 minutes. You might find it helpful to set an alarm to remind you when to stop.
Step 5: Move on to something else	When Thinking Time is over, it's time to move on to another activity that can help take your mind away from your worries and lift your mood, such as exercise, listening to music or calling a friend. Try to do this with as much attention as possible.

Arjun says: I was surprised how helpful it was to do Thinking Time. It especially helped me at night because I kept a notebook by my bed, and it was much easier to get back to sleep if I made a quick note of any worries during the night rather than lying awake and worrying for ages. After a few days of regular practice, when it came to Thinking Time, I would sometimes find I didn't even have that much to worry about! Doing this regularly has helped me to cut down on how long I spend thinking about problems.

Summary: worry

→ Worry can be triggered by major life problems or by the stresses of daily life.

→ Getting stuck on the Worry Roundabout involves thinking endlessly about distressing or difficult problems and can make you feel anxious, low and unable to relax.

→ It's common to have 'What if…?' thoughts about bad things in the future that may never really happen.

→ Worry actions include asking for reassurance, procrastination, avoiding situations that cause worry or pushing yourself to over-prepare and prevent any possible mistakes.

→ You can use Noticing the NOW and Thinking Time to help cut down how much time you spend worrying each day.

Final thoughts

Make a note of anything you have found helpful, interesting or surprising from this chapter.

....

....

....

....

....

....

What are you going to do now? Can you choose one small action for the coming week based on what you have read so far?

....

....

....

....

....

....

Chapter 8

SHYNESS AND SOCIAL ANXIETY

Imani: I've always been shy, but I used to have a small group of close friends that I'd known for a long time and felt safe with. Last year we moved house and I started going to a bigger school where I found it very hard to make new friends. Every day before school, I would get really worried that I might say something stupid and make a fool of myself. When anyone spoke to me, I would start stuttering and my face would go bright red. In groups, I just kept very quiet and I'm sure most people thought I was boring. Even if someone invited me to go out with them, I would say no because I didn't want to look foolish or embarrass myself. I spent a lot of time by myself in my room and it started to feel very lonely. It was starting to get me down.

It's common to sometimes feel self-conscious, nervous or shy in front of others, especially in stressful situations such as public speaking or during an interview. But, if your feelings of anxiety have become more intense, or your worries about being judged negatively, criticized or looking foolish in front of other people are making it hard to speak up about things that matter to you, or you are missing out on important life experiences because of these fears, then it may be time to work on your social anxiety.

In this chapter, we will explore:

➜ what kinds of situations can trigger social anxiety

➜ how social anxiety can affect your thoughts, feelings and body

➜ a quick skill to use when you are feeling anxious in social situations.

 Read This 5 Minutes

What is social anxiety?

Social anxiety involves fear of doing something embarrassing in front of other people that would make them think negatively of you or judge you harshly. It is more than just shyness. It can be very distressing and have a big impact on your life, affecting relationships, school, work and many other activities. It can cause anxiety in many common situations such as speaking in a large group, performing in front of others or meeting new people.

Social anxiety is often triggered by worries about doing something embarrassing or humiliating such as blushing, sweating, making a mistake or appearing boring, weird or stupid to other people. You might also find it hard to do things when others are watching. You may be afraid that people will think badly of you or that you won't be as good as others.

The good news is that you can learn to be more comfortable in social situations and stop allowing social anxiety to get in the way of doing important things.

 Pause and Think   10 Minutes

Do you feel anxious in social situations?

What social situations do you find most difficult? Complete the following activity to think about the situations or activities that are most likely to make you feel anxious or fearful.

Types of social situations	Tick if this causes anxiety	What examples can you think of?
Having a one-to-one conversation		
Being in a large group of people		

Going to a party or a social gathering		
Meeting new people		
Going on a date or asking someone out		
Speaking up in class or in front of others		
Talking to someone in authority such as a teacher or headteacher		
Being the centre of attention		
Performing in front of others, such as getting on stage or playing an instrument		
Eating or drinking in front of others		
Being observed or watched when carrying out an activity		
Making a phone call		
Sitting in a public area such as on a bus or train		
What other social or performance situations cause you anxiety?		

If you have ticked yes to three of more of these questions, then it may be time to work on your social anxiety.

 Read This  10 Minutes

Understanding social anxiety

We can explore how social anxiety can affect your body, mind and emotions using an Anxiety Map.

The anxiety passengers change your thinking and you:
• exaggerate the danger
• focus on everything that could go wrong
• keep going over and over the problem
• believe you can't cope so you lose confidence.

There are changes in your body such as: shaking, sweating, muscle tension, rapid breathing, racing heart, feeling sick.

In your body

Situation and triggers

What you think

What you feel

Your actions

You might feel: fearful, anxious, scared, worried, afraid, panicky or overwhelmed.

You carry out anxiety actions such as:
Fight – get angry or irritable
Flight – leave places that make you anxious
Freeze – put off or cut down activities
Find safety – avoid or put off things that make you anxious, check and double-check, ask for reassurance.

 **Read This** **3 Minutes**

Feelings

Social anxiety can lead to many uncomfortable feelings and emotions which can occur before, during or after a social situation. You might start to feel anxious, worried, fearful or even have a panic attack. There may be feelings of embarrassment or shame. Over time, you can lose confidence in your ability to cope in social situations. You may start to feel fed up and low if you become isolated or are struggling to do things that are important to you because of social anxiety.

Pause and Think **3 Minutes**

How does social anxiety make you feel? What emotions can you notice?

....

....

....

 Read This **3 Minutes**

Physical symptoms

The sense of threat and danger in social situations can trigger your Threat system and you might find that your Anxiety Alarm starts to sound very loudly!

This leads to the Fight Flight Freeze reaction which can bring many different physical symptoms and body sensations. Remember, these physical reactions are designed to help you fight the danger, run away or stay still and remain safe. They might feel quite unpleasant for a while but are not dangerous or harmful.

 Pause and Think **5 Minutes**

Body changes during social anxiety

Use this activity to explore what body changes you notice when you are anxious in social situations.

What happens in your body	Can you recognize this? What do you notice?
Trembling or shaking	
Blushing or heat in your face	

cont.

What happens in your body	Can you recognize this? What do you notice?
Pounding or racing heart	
Feeling sick or churning stomach	
Feeling hot or sweaty	
Feeling dizzy or light-headed	
Mind going blank or feeling frozen or stuck	
Fast breathing or a tight chest	
Dry mouth or a lump in your throat	
Finding it hard to concentrate or focus	

Imani says: I have lots of changes in my body in social situations. My heart starts to thump fast in my chest, and I feel hot. I blush bright red and start sweating. I have such a dry mouth that it feels impossible to speak. I get really worried that everyone will notice how anxious I am. It's really embarrassing.

 Read This  10 Minutes

Thoughts in social anxiety

If you get anxious in social situations, then you might have scary or upsetting thoughts about what might go wrong. These thoughts can involve past, present or future events. These thoughts may appear as words, or you might also have distressing pictures or images in your mind where you see yourself looking foolish or others pointing and laughing at you. You will often focus on the worst-case scenarios, which can lead to thoughts such as:

When you are in a social situation, you might also have lots of thoughts and worries about how you appear to others. Perhaps you see yourself blushing furiously, stumbling over your words, shaking or pouring with sweat.

The Anxiety Train passengers will often show up and exaggerate how severe or noticeable these symptoms are. They might tell you how badly you are performing and that others can notice, saying things like:

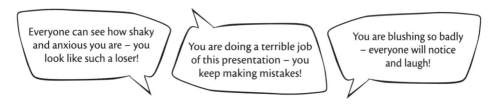

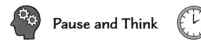 **Pause and Think** 5 Minutes

What anxious thoughts do you have in social situations?

Use this table to explore the thoughts that you experience during social situations which might trigger feelings of anxiety.

What kinds of anxious thoughts, fears or worries do you have in social situations?	
What exaggerated or unhelpful stories do the Anxiety Train passengers tell you?	
What images or pictures come into your mind?	
How do you imagine that you appear to other people? Are there any changes in your body that you believe are obvious to others?	

Imani says: I have lots of anxious thoughts whenever I am in a social situation. I worry a lot about how others see me. I always think the worst and believe that other people will think I'm boring or stupid. I often have a picture of myself as a shaky, sweating wreck with a bright red face! These worries are starting to affect me and I'm feeling quite isolated and lonely.

 **Read This**  5 Minutes

Your actions and social anxiety

Avoiding social situations

If social situations make you feel anxious, then you might react by trying to avoid or escape from them to feel better. This is understandable but, unfortunately, it can often make things worse. Avoiding social situations may provide some short-term relief from anxiety, but you will also lose confidence in your ability to cope in social situations, so your anxiety only grows stronger with time.

Avoiding social situations due to anxiety can also stop you from doing many important and enjoyable things. You might become isolated and cut off from friends, or unable to participate in activities where you might need to speak up in public or be observed by others.

 Pause and Think **5 Minutes**

What are you avoiding due to social anxiety?

What situations are you avoiding due to social anxiety? What important activities are you missing out on because of fears or worries about how you may be seen by other people?

....
....
....
....
....
....
....

 **Read This** **5 Minutes**

Safety-seeking actions

When it's not possible to avoid a social situation then you might choose actions that help you to feel safer or more comfortable in the situation such as staying close to someone safe, avoiding eye contact or being very quiet in a social group.

It may feel like these actions are helping but, like avoidance, they can make social anxiety worse over time. Safety-seeking actions prevent you from facing your fears about scary social situations. This stops you from discovering that the worst is unlikely to happen, that the situation is safe and you can cope socially.

Pause and Think **5 Minutes**

Which of the following safety-seeking actions do you use to help you cope with social situations?

Safety-seeking actions	Do you recognize this?	What examples can you think of?
Looking down or avoiding eye contact		
Staying quiet or hiding in the background to escape notice		
Making excuses to leave early		
Only talking to people that you feel safe with		
Wearing clothes that mean you will not stand out or be noticed		
Using make up to cover blushing		
Over-preparing for lessons or presentations in class		
Thinking about or mentally rehearsing what you are going to say		
Staying close to someone who feels safe		
Using alcohol or drugs to help you cope		

 **Read This** **10 Minutes**

Attention and focus

When you are anxious in a social situation, it's easy to get stuck in your head. Perhaps you find it impossible to stop thinking about how everyone is staring and judging you. You may be busy mentally planning and rehearsing what to say next, or thinking about your anxious body sensations, focusing on your flushed cheeks, sweaty hands or racing heart, either trying to control them or work out how noticeable they are to others.

You might also find yourself looking around for possible problems, perhaps looking for signs that you are being criticized or judged negatively by other people. If people nearby are smiling, then you might assume that they are laughing at you. If someone frowns, yawns or looks at their phone, you may think this means they are bored or uninterested in what you are saying. This constant search for threats can leave you feeling stressed and tense, and you might ignore or simply not notice all the positive feedback from others, such as encouraging looks, smiles and friendly expressions.

Focusing too much attention on your anxious thoughts, feelings and body sensations will usually make you feel even worse and can make it harder to cope in social situations. Getting stuck in your mind stops you from listening or paying attention to a conversation, making it harder to get involved. You might miss someone asking you a question, or not notice when it's your turn to speak. It's harder to think of something interesting or relevant to say if you are busy worrying about whether you seem anxious or whether the other person is bored. All this can make you believe that you are not very socially skilled – when it's simply that you are just not paying attention.

 **Pause and Think** **5 Minutes**

Where is your attention in social situations?

Use this activity to think about where you focus your attention during social situations.

Where is your attention when you are in a social situation? Do you get stuck in your head – caught up in thoughts and worries, or notice unpleasant emotions or body sensations?	

Do you spend a lot of time looking around for signs that others are thinking badly of you in some way?	
Do you spend a lot of time planning or rehearsing what you are going to say?	
What's the impact of this? Does it affect how well you can listen or get involved in conversations with others?	

 **Read This**  **5 Minutes**

Social anxiety tips

Here are some quick tips for dealing with social anxiety:

Your thoughts are not facts! It's common to have extreme or negative unhelpful beliefs that focus on things that have gone wrong and assume that other people are thinking the worst about you. But having these thoughts does not make them true or accurate. Things are rarely as bad as you might imagine. It's just the Anxiety Train passengers showing up –you don't have to believe everything they say!

Your anxiety is not as obvious as you fear. Most people with social anxiety have an inaccurate view of how they appear to others. Even though you may feel anxious, it's likely that others cannot see it as much as you fear. Other people are far more likely to be worrying about their performance than thinking about what you say or do.

It's OK to seem a little nervous! Even if someone notices that you're nervous, it doesn't mean they'll think badly of you. Other people will often be feeling just as nervous as you are. Try not to judge yourself too harshly or expect yourself to be completely free of anxiety in social or performance situations. Things will often improve if you accept your anxiety and give yourself some time and space to settle into the situation.

Let go of the pressure to be perfect. It's fine to trip over the odd word, have a period of silence in the conversation or have a red face sometimes. What's important is to focus on being kind and genuine and to pay attention to the people around you. People will appreciate these qualities and notice them. They are unlikely to focus on every word that you say or to expect your conversation to be word-perfect.

Face your fears. You can overcome your fear of social situations by gradually starting to face them and taking things one small step at a time. Start with a situation that feels just outside your comfort zone and gradually work up to bigger challenges as you build your confidence and coping skills. We talk more about ways to step out of the Safety Zone and face your fears in Chapter 12.

 Read This   3 Minutes

Keep your attention on track

A simple but effective skill to help you cope better with social anxiety is to practise paying attention to what's happening in the 'here and now' during a conversation. It can help you to shift your attention away from negative thoughts, feelings and body sensations, and become more involved and enjoy social activities more.

You can start to notice when you are stuck in your thoughts, feelings and body sensations, and then make an effort to bring your focus and attention to the conversation at hand. This involves listening closely to what the other person is saying and then switching to your ideas and opinions when it's your turn to speak.

 Do This   5 Minutes

Have a focused conversation

Choose someone that you feel comfortable talking to and agree on a time to have a conversation. Before the conversation, take a few slow breaths and remind yourself that it's OK to feel anxious in social situations. Then talk to the person for 5–10 minutes while you pay attention to what they are saying.

Use the following steps:

- → **Look** at the person when they are talking. Notice their facial expressions and body posture.

- → **Listen** to their tone of voice and the words they are saying.

- → **Repeat** back at least one statement that the person has said. 'So, you are saying that...' This will help you to focus on what they are saying and shows that you are listening.

- → **Ask** a question that is relevant to the topic of conversation.

- → **Say** your own opinion. Don't be afraid to add to the conversation with your thoughts and ideas.

If you notice your mind wandering or getting distracted, gently bring it back to the conversation. Don't get frustrated or give yourself a hard time if you find this difficult at first. It's a skill that you can learn with time and patience. It's important to practise regularly – so try it for a few minutes every day if you can.

Once you have built up your confidence, try using this skill in other conversations. Start small and with one-to-one discussions with people you know well. Eventually, you can work towards building your confidence with larger groups or with people you are less familiar with.

We talk more about strengthening your attention muscle in Chapter 13 and you can redo the exercises in this chapter to help develop your confidence in social situations.

Imani says: I was shocked to discover how much time I spent in my head whenever I was in a social situation! I was spending so much time worrying about what to say, which made it difficult to listen to what was going on around me. I decided to practise having a focused conversation with my best friend. Even then, I found that my mind kept drifting back to thoughts and worries about what I was saying and whether it was OK. I tried hard to bring my attention back to listening to Sara and, after a while, it was easier to keep focused on what she was saying. I'm going to keep practising and maybe try with someone I don't know so well next time.

Summary: social anxiety

- → Social anxiety involves fear of doing something embarrassing in front of other people that would make them think negatively or judge you harshly.

→ Avoiding situations that trigger social anxiety can make you lose confidence and miss out on important activities.

→ Being stuck in your head during social situations makes it harder to listen or be involved.

→ Letting go of the pressure to do things perfectly and allowing yourself to feel a little anxious can make it easier to cope.

→ Keeping your attention on track involves focusing on the person you are talking to.

Final thoughts

Make a note of anything you have found helpful, interesting or surprising from this chapter.

....

....

....

....

....

....

What are you going to do now? Can you choose one small action for the coming week based on what you have read so far?

....

....

....

....

....

....

Chapter 9

HEALTH ANXIETY

William: I've always worried about my health, but things got much worse last year after I found out my uncle was being treated for cancer. He's always seemed so strong and fit, and I started thinking that if he could get sick then maybe I would too. Whenever I had a headache, I would start feeling anxious that it was due to something terrible like a brain tumour or a bleed in my brain. If I got a cold or a runny nose, I was convinced that it would develop into pneumonia or a serious infection. I kept asking my parents to take me to the doctor who would check me over and tell me I was fine. I'd feel better for a while but then I'd notice something new like an ache in my leg or a gurgling tummy and my anxiety would be just as bad as ever.

We all get ill from time to time, and it's completely normal to have concerns about your health or about people you care about. But sometimes worries about health can grow into a bigger problem that has a major effect on how you live your life. It can affect your relationships with family and friends, whether you can work or study, and alter your mood and emotions.

In this next chapter, we will explore:

➜ what health anxiety is and how it affects your body and mind

➜ some quick tips for coping with health anxiety

➜ one important skill for stopping health worries from taking over your life.

 **Read This** **10 Minutes**

What is health anxiety?

Health anxiety involves becoming very anxious or worried that you might have, or develop, a serious illness. These worries are often out of proportion and exaggerated, but they can feel very real and scary.

Health anxiety can occur in healthy people. You might continue to feel anxious even after having negative tests or being told by a doctor or a nurse that everything is OK, or the reassurance may help for a short while but then the anxiety starts to come back.

Health anxiety can also occur in people who are living with illnesses or long-term conditions such as asthma or diabetes. You might find it hard to cope with the uncertainty of having the condition and the changes that it brings to your life or find it hard to stop worrying about developing another illness.

It is important to emphasize that health worries are not 'all in your head' and that your symptoms and body sensations are real. Whether you have a health problem is *not* the main issue in health anxiety.

The problem is that the symptoms are having such a big impact on your life, and the ways you are coping with them may be making things worse. Constantly thinking and worrying about your health, checking your body for possible illness or repeatedly seeking medical tests or reassurance can lead to more stress and anxiety. If these thoughts and behaviours are distressing or getting in the way of living an enjoyable life, then it may be time to work on your health anxiety.

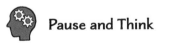 **Pause and Think**  **10 Minutes**

Is health anxiety a problem for you?

Look at this checklist to see if you are having problems with health anxiety.

Possible signs of health anxiety	Is this true for you? What examples can you think of?
Do you worry a lot about your health or find it hard to stop thinking about it?	
Do you often think that body sensations might be a sign of a serious health problem?	
Does worrying about your health stop you from doing other things that are important or fun?	
Do you often check your body for signs that something might be wrong?	
Do you often visit a doctor or nurse to discuss your health concerns or to get tests or a check-up?	
Do you continue to worry about your health even if others have reassured you that all is well?	
Do you spend a lot of time looking for information about your symptoms or illnesses online or in books?	
Do you talk about your health a lot with your family or friends?	
Do you avoid any situations or places because they might trigger worries about your health?	

If three or more of these questions apply to you, then it may be time to work on your health anxiety.

 Read This 🕐 3 Minutes

Understanding health anxiety

We can explore how health anxiety can affect your body, mind and emotions using an Anxiety Map.

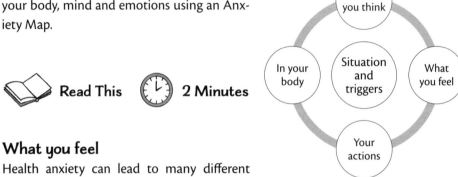

 Read This 🕐 2 Minutes

What you feel

Health anxiety can lead to many different feelings and emotions. You might feel anxious and fearful, edgy or irritable. Feeling anxious for a long time can also make you feel fed up and sad or low. You might also feel angry or frustrated, perhaps with yourself or your body, or with others if you feel they are not taking your concerns seriously or are unable to help.

🧠 Pause and Think 🕐 5 Minutes

What feelings or emotions can you notice when you are worried about your health?

....

....

....

....

....

 **Read This**  **3 Minutes**

In your body

Health anxiety can be linked to many different body sensations and symptoms. You can worry about *any* physical symptom, whether it's new or you have had it for a long time.

When you feel anxious that there may be something wrong with your health, this will trigger your Threat system and set off the Fight Flight Freeze response. This can lead to even more body symptoms and sensations such as feeling tired, having muscle pain, sleep problems, headaches or tummy pain, which you may then also start to worry about.

 Pause and Think **5 Minutes**

What body sensations or symptoms are likely to trigger your health anxiety? Do you have any anxiety symptoms caused by the Threat system setting off your Fight Flight Freeze response?

....
....
....
....
....

 Read This **5 Minutes**

Thoughts and health anxiety

It's common to have lots of thoughts and worries about health and illness. You might fear developing a particular illness, such as cancer, a mental health condition or a heart problem. Or you might have vague worries about something bad happening or getting ill in some way without being sure what might happen. You might be worried that a health professional has made a mistake or missed a serious health problem. You might also have scary thoughts that your family or loved ones could get seriously ill or even die.

The health Anxiety Train passengers are very likely to show up in your mind when you are stuck in worries about health and illness. They will focus on the most severe illnesses and will insist that you are going to develop the most serious and scary health problems, saying things such as:

> What if the doctor has made a mistake or missed something?

> It's been going on for ages, that must be bad.

> What if this cold turns into pneumonia and you die?

> You've got another headache – could it be a brain tumour?

> Does this pain mean that there's something seriously wrong?

 Pause and Think **5 Minutes**

Use this table to think about the different thoughts or worries that you have about health.

What worry thoughts come into your mind when thinking about your health?	
Are there any symptoms that you worry about most?	

Is there a particular health problem or illness that you are concerned you may have or develop in the future?	
Do you worry about the health of someone close to you and fear the worst?	
What do the health Anxiety Train passengers tell you? What's the scariest part about this? What do you imagine will happen?	

 Pause and Think **10 Minutes**

Health anxiety actions

When you worry a lot about health, you might carry out anxiety actions to try to make yourself feel better. However, just like with other types of anxiety, these actions can often make things worse and keep you feeling anxious and stuck.

Look at this list of health anxiety actions and make a note of any that you recognize.

Health anxiety action	Do you recognize this? What do you do when worrying about your health?
Do you often check your body looking for new or changing symptoms or signs of illness?	
Do you spend a lot of time looking at health information online or in the media?	
Does health anxiety make you visit a doctor or nurse about your health more often than you need to?	

cont.

Health anxiety action	Do you recognize this? What do you do when worrying about your health?
Does thinking or worrying about your health distract you or get in the way of doing other things that may be important or enjoyable?	
Do you often ask for reassurance from others that you are not ill?	
Do you try to avoid thinking about health so that you don't trigger health worries? Do you avoid going to see the doctor or watching medical TV programmes?	
Do you act as if you could be ill, such as by cutting down on physical activity?	
Have you stopped or reduced doing anything important because of your health worries?	

 Read This  5 Minutes

The effects of health anxiety actions

While these health anxiety actions are understandable and common, they can also cause some big problems. Constantly poking and prodding your body and checking for possible illness can cause aches and pains which make you even more worried. You might also notice things in your body which have always been there, but you start worrying that they may be new or different.

Constantly asking for reassurance that you are well from friends, family or health professionals may reduce your anxiety for a short while, but it can also make you gradually lose confidence and lead to an even stronger fear that something serious may be wrong.

Spending a lot of time online looking up your symptoms and what they might mean is also unhelpful. You are likely to find out all kinds of scary information which makes you feel worse. Doing this also keeps your mind focused on your health rather than thinking about other things that are interesting, fun or enjoyable. Cutting down on important activities can make life feel flat and make you feel fed up and low.

 Pause and Think  **5 Minutes**

How do these actions affect you?

What's the effect of all these health anxiety actions on your life and your mood and happiness? How often are you doing them? You might find it helpful to keep a diary of how often you are carrying out each one over a week or two.

....

....

....

....

....

Health anxiety tips

Here are some quick tips for dealing with health anxiety:

Body sensations are normal! Your body is constantly sending you messages and information which will lead to sensations such as aches, tingling or soreness. It's normal and healthy to experience all these feelings – they are not just signs of serious illness or disease.

It's impossible to diagnose yourself. When you are worried about a health problem, you will often find yourself seeking out more and more information about it, often by looking it up online. Unfortunately, this will often lead to the discovery of even more scary possibilities and is likely to make you feel worse rather than better. The internet doesn't know anything about you and not all sites are accurate or a good source of information.

Anxious thoughts about your health are not facts! Just because the Anxiety Train passengers are telling you that 'It must be cancer!' or that 'You are going to die!' does not mean they are correct. You don't have to believe everything that they say. They will always focus on the scariest and worst possible causes of your symptoms.

Worry cannot keep you healthy. Spending a lot of time thinking or worrying about getting ill will not stop the worst from happening, but it can make you feel anxious and unhappy. It's important that the *fear* of illness doesn't stop you from living your life and being able to enjoy yourself.

Get back to the things you care about. Rather than allowing health anxiety to dominate your life, can you gradually start doing more things that you care about? Can you get back to doing anything that you have been avoiding due to your health worries, such as seeing friends or doing sports and other activities?

If thoughts or worries about your health are making you start to feel extremely anxious or panicky, then you can also use the 54321 technique that we introduced in Chapter 6.

 Do This  10 Minutes

Swap anxiety actions for doing something fun or interesting

It's easy to get caught up in endlessly searching for information online about health and your symptoms, but this will only keep you stuck on the health anxiety Worry Roundabout. You are more likely to find out scary information and spend way too much time thinking about health rather than other things that are important in life.

The alternative is to do something else with your time. Try some different actions and see what the impact is on your life and your mood as you build back up to doing some things that you've cut down on because of health anxiety.

Cut down on these actions	Try these actions instead	How can you use this? What will you try?
Reduce how much time you spend looking up your symptoms on the internet or searching online for health information.	Step away from the computer and try doing something you know is good for your wellbeing – physical activity or another interest or hobby that you enjoy. Phone a friend and have a chat, meet up or kick a ball around the park.	
Cut back on checking your body for signs of illness such as lumps, tingling or pain.	Keep your hands occupied by doing a craft such as painting, drawing or carving, or try building something from Lego, practise creative writing or play a musical instrument. Stroke your pet to help soothe yourself.	

Stop reading scary health-related news stories.	Scroll past health-related news stories and pick something else to focus on. What's the latest celebrity gossip, or what's happening to your favourite sports team? Find out something new about a topic that you are interested in and enjoy learning about.	

William says: When I stop and think I can see what a massive impact health anxiety has had on my life. I spend so much of my day thinking and worrying about getting ill that it's starting to get me down. It was helpful to learn about the health anxiety actions because I think I do nearly all of these and they take up a lot of time and energy. I'm going to try and cut down on googling my symptoms. It will be hard because when I'm anxious, I do feel a strong urge to look at my phone, but I know it doesn't help – it just makes me feel worse! I'm going to try and do something else instead. I'll try going for a jog or even just a walk around the block, which might help. I want to get back to doing things I was enjoying before my uncle got ill. I know he wouldn't want me to miss out. I might try to get back to my martial arts class next week…

Summary: health anxiety

➜ Health anxiety involves fear and worry that you may develop a serious illness.

➜ Unhelpful actions such as frequent body checking and repeatedly googling your symptoms can make your anxiety worse.

➜ It's normal to have body sensations – they don't automatically mean you have a serious illness.

➜ You can choose helpful ways to respond when you have health worries, such as getting back to doing activities you care about.

Final thoughts

Make a note of anything you have found helpful, interesting or surprising from this chapter.

....

....

....

....

....

....

What are you going to do now? Can you choose one small action for the coming week based on what you have read so far?

....

....

....

....

....

....

Part 3

SIX GROWTH STEPS TO BEAT ANXIETY AND PANIC

Chapter 10

WHAT ARE THE GROWTH STEPS?

In this chapter, we will meet the six 10-minute GROWTH steps that can help you beat anxiety and panic. We will look at each step in more detail in the following chapters. These steps don't have to be followed in order. You might also need to go back and forth between chapters several times as you face new situations, challenges or stressful situations.

Here's an overview of the 10-minute GROWTH steps:

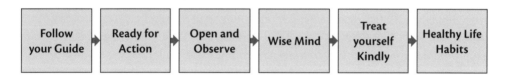

| Follow your Guide | Ready for Action | Open and Observe | Wise Mind | Treat yourself Kindly | Healthy Life Habits |

📖 Read This   🕐 5 Minutes

Follow your Guide

The first step is to meet your Guide. This is like an inner compass that points towards the things in life that are most important to you and that you care about. Following your Guide involves asking yourself 'Who and what do I care about? What kind of person do I want to be? What do I want out of life? Is what I am doing right now leading me in that direction?'

You will meet your Guide in Chapter 11 where you will start to explore some of the things that motivate and interest you.

Ready for Action

Being Ready for Action involves changing what you do and how you act. Doing more activities that are important or enjoyable can help to lift your mood, increase your energy and happiness, and help to distract you from anxiety or worries. Getting Ready for Action involves planning and completing small actions that follow the direction in which your Guide is pointing.

Sometimes, you may feel unsure what to try, so you can experiment by trying things out, testing how it feels to do them, discovering what happens and whether they fit with who you want to be. You don't have to be certain what the outcome will be, and it may take time and many tiny steps to achieve an important life goal.

You will start getting Ready for Action by setting yourself some small goals to do things that matter to you in Chapter 12.

Open and Observe

Learning to Open and Observe involves noticing what's going on inside you and in the world around you. Being able to recognize your thoughts, feelings and actions can help you to understand yourself, make sense of how you are reacting in any situation, and decide whether these reactions are helpful or unhelpful. It might involve tuning in to what you feel in your body and noticing your thoughts, feelings and urges to react in certain ways. It also involves appreciating what is here and now, rather than worrying about things in the future or churning over events from the past. This is a useful skill that can help you deal with uncomfortable feelings of anxiety, cope better under pressure, feel less overwhelmed and find it easier to follow your Guide and do more things that you care about.

You will start practising Open and Observe skills in Chapter 13.

Wise Mind

Your mind is your inner voice and includes your thoughts, beliefs, ideas, expectations, memories and personal stories. It is an incredibly powerful and useful tool that can allow you to make complicated decisions and plans. However, at other times, your mind may slip into anxious thinking habits, where you spend a lot of time worrying about problems that may never happen, exaggerating the risks and convincing yourself that something really bad is going to happen. If your mind is stuck on the Anxiety Train, you can end up feeling constantly fearful, tense and panicky, and it can drain your confidence and self-belief.

Using Wise Mind involves learning to look at the bigger picture and decide if your thoughts are balanced and helpful. You can learn to step back from negative thoughts and pause before acting on impulse. You can also learn how to tune out from unhelpful thinking patterns that may be keeping you stuck, draining your confidence and making it harder to get past feelings of fear or anxiety. You can learn to notice more helpful thoughts, such as focusing on what's most important to you and remembering your strengths and good qualities, and allow these to influence your actions and choices.

You will discover more about your Wise Mind in Chapter 14.

Treat yourself Kindly

Are you supportive, friendly and encouraging to yourself or do you give yourself a hard time and get stuck in self-criticism and blame? Learning to Treat yourself Kindly involves being kind, friendly and fair to yourself, and balancing three different emotion systems which all have an important part to play in your health and happiness:

→ **Threat system:** This will alert you to possible danger and help you quickly take action to stay safe, but if you overuse this system, you can feel anxious, stressed and agitated.

→ **Drive system:** This energizes and motivates you, helping you seek out opportunities and achieve your goals. If you don't use this system effectively you can feel demotivated and fed up and find it hard to get important things done.

→ **Calm and Connect system:** This helps you feel peaceful, contented, calm and safe. It helps you to feel close to other people and to recover when facing problems or when things go wrong. If you don't use this system enough, you can become self-critical and give yourself a hard time when coping with problems or difficult situations.

You will discover how to balance these systems and banish your self-critic in Chapter 15.

Healthy Life Habits

Building Healthy Life Habits involves making choices about your daily routines that will make you feel happier, more energetic, less anxious and more able to achieve the things that are important to you. This includes being active, having healthy eating patterns, getting enough sleep, cutting back on unhealthy choices such as alcohol or drugs, and taking good care of health conditions or illness.

We will explore Healthy Life Habits more in Chapter 16.

 **Pause and Think**  **5 Minutes**

What's next?

What do you take away from this brief introduction to the six GROWTH steps? Did any steps feel particularly important for you? If so, you can jump to that chapter next.

If not, we recommend that you start with Chapter 11, which will introduce your Guide. This is often a helpful starting point that can build your motivation and help you focus on what you care about.

Summary: overview of the GROWTH steps

This chapter introduced the six 10-minute GROWTH steps:

→ **G**uide: Focus on who you want to be and what you care about most.

→ **R**eady for Action: Prepare for change and take small steps towards what matters.

→ **O**pen and **O**bserve: Be more aware of what's going on in your mind, body and the world around you.

→ **W**ise Mind: Get perspective and choose helpful ways to react to different situations.

→ **T**reat yourself Kindly: Balance your emotion systems and banish your inner critic.

→ **H**ealthy Life Habits: Create healthy routines that encourage your wellbeing.

Final thoughts

Make a note of anything you have found helpful, interesting or surprising from this chapter.

....

....

....

....

....

....

What are you going to do now? Can you choose one small action based on what you have discovered from this chapter?

....

....

....

....

....

....

Chapter 11

FOLLOW YOUR GUIDE

Meera: Anxiety affects so many parts of my life and I've been left feeling quite lost and uncertain. I find it hard to make decisions because I'm anxious about making the wrong choice, so I often end up not doing anything. I keep questioning and second-guessing myself and feeling out of control. If something small goes wrong, I will tend to focus on this and lose the confidence to try anything else. Feeling anxious in social situations has cut me off from a lot of people and I'm more isolated than I used to be. It's like I don't know who I am anymore.

Who or what is your Guide?

When you feel anxious, you may lose confidence in yourself, which leads to cutting down on many activities that used to make life feel fun or create a sense of purpose. As we learned in Chapter 3, living with anxiety will often lead to actions such as avoiding situations that make you anxious, procrastination over important tasks, trying to avoid feelings of anxiety by distracting yourself with technology or even turning to drugs or alcohol. All of these actions can move you away from the things that matter to you and can leave you feeling lost and confused.

This is where your Guide can help. Your Guide is like an inner compass that points in the direction of the people and things that are important to you. Following your Guide can help you make decisions and choose actions that help you to reclaim your life and feel more fulfilled, contented and self-confident.

Finding your Guide involves thinking about your personal **values** – what matters most to you at a deeper level and what connects you to others. It involves discovering what is important to you and what gives your life **meaning** and **purpose**. Following your Guide includes choosing **actions** that take you in the direction you wish your life to go so that you are living in line with your values, even if this involves effort and overcoming challenges or feelings of anxiety.

In this chapter, we will meet your personal Guide and discover:

➜ what is most important to you

➜ what direction your Guide is pointing in

➜ how your Guide can help you to increase your confidence and overcome feeling lost or confused in your life

➜ how you can start doing more things that matter even when you are feeling anxious or fearful.

 Pause and Think **5 Minutes**

What is important to you?

Getting to know your Guide involves asking yourself some 'big' questions. Look at some of these below:

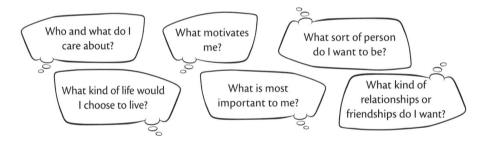

What immediately comes to mind? Don't worry about getting the 'right' answer, as there will be lots of chances to change and develop your ideas throughout the book.

Write your first thoughts here:

....

....

....

....

....

 Read This   10 Minutes

Why do values matter?

It can be a challenge to deal with the many different pressures, stresses and changes that you may be facing in life. There might be demands to study or pass exams, along-side keeping up with extracurricular activities and hobbies. You may be dealing with social pressures and wanting to fit in, changes in your body and your sense of who you are, and many different types of life problems.

Thinking about your values can help you choose how to live, even when life is tough when the challenges may seem huge and your anxiety may be skyrocketing. This is exactly when it can be most important to follow your Guide. When you are feeling fearful, stuck, confused or overwhelmed, you can turn to your Guide to motivate and inspire yourself to make helpful choices and keep going when facing life's difficulties.

Knowing your values can help you to make choices that fit with who you want to be as a person. If you value friendship, kindness or social connection, it's worth making the effort to meet up with a friend who is struggling, even when you are anxious and stressed about some upcoming exams or coursework. If you value physical exercise or the outdoors, it becomes worth the effort to get outside and go for a cycle ride or a walk, even when you are feeling anxious and overwhelmed by worries about an argument with your friend.

What are your values?

Take a few minutes to look at this list of values. Rate how important each one is to you from 1–5 (where 1 is not very important and 5 is extremely important). Aim for around 4–6 very important values (scoring 4 or 5) at the moment.

Remember, values are personal and no one is judging your choices. You can change your choices at any time if they do not seem a good 'fit'. You can also add any important values that you think are missing from the list. If you are finding it hard to choose, imagine being on a boat that is sinking, and you can only keep a handful of your values, tossing the rest overboard. Which would you choose to hang onto?

Values	How important? (1-5)	Values	How important? (1–5)
ACCEPTANCE: being accepted for who you are and accepting others		**INDEPENDENCE:** being able to make your own decisions and choices	

cont.

Values	How important? (1-5)	Values	How important? (1–5)
ACHIEVEMENT: making progress towards important accomplishments and goals		**INDIVIDUALITY:** to express yourself as a unique person, celebrating diversity and difference	
ACKNOWLEDGEMENT: to matter, to be appreciated, seen and heard by others		**KINDNESS:** being friendly, caring and encouraging to yourself and others	
ACTIVE: participating in physical activities, exercise, dance, movement or sports		**RELATIONSHIPS:** having close personal, romantic and/or sexual relationships	
ADVENTURE: having new and exciting experiences		**LEADERSHIP:** taking responsibility for making decisions and guiding others	
BELONGING: feeling part of a friendship group, community, team, organization, culture and family		**LEARN and GROW:** making progress, developing skills and discovering new knowledge	
BODY and HEALTH: taking care of your body, health and appearance		**NATURE:** the outdoors, animals and the natural world	
CALM: finding peace and tranquillity in your life		**ORDER:** being organized, following or developing a pattern or routine	
CARE: looking after yourself and others		**SAFETY:** finding physical and emotional safety, security and predictability	
CHALLENGE: solving problems, stretching your limits and testing your abilities		**SPACE:** finding freedom, reducing restrictions and demands in your life	
CONNECTION: affection, warmth and closeness with important people in your life		**SPIRITUALITY and RELIGION:** following important beliefs and traditions	
CONTRIBUTION: giving your time and using your skills in ways that feel important or meaningful		**TEAMWORK:** working in a group with shared goals	

CREATIVITY: expressing or enjoying creativity in different ways, including music, writing and art		**TRUST:** honesty, fairness and being able to trust those around you	
FINANCE: having security and money to spend as you choose		**VARIETY:** seeking out new and different experiences	
FUN: humour, laughter and enjoyment		**WORLD MATTERS:** politics, global or environmental issues	
Other important values? List these here:		Other important values? List these here:	

 Pause and Think **5 Minutes**

Did you find it easy or difficult to choose your values? Was it hard to stick to only 4–6 important values, or did very few seem right for you?

....
....
....

How does it feel to think about your values? Have you discovered anything important or useful?

....
....
....

Meera: I found it quite hard to pick my values at first because I kept changing my mind and I didn't want to choose the wrong ones! In the end, I went back and tried to remind myself that it's OK to pick some values for now, but I can always change these again if something else becomes more important. I realized that my friends are really important to me, and I also would like there to be more fun and enjoyment in life. I also picked creativity because I've always enjoyed crafts and making things. The final value I chose that is very important to me is challenge. I want to be able to challenge myself more and stop anxiety from ruling my life.

 **Read This** **5 Minutes**

Key facts about values

Here's a quick reminder of some important facts about values and your Guide.

Values are...	Values are not...
✓ Directions not destinations. Values focus on the journey and the route that you travel, not the outcome.	✗ Goals to achieve or things to tick off your to-do list.
✓ Flexible ideas that change over time as you grow and develop and can be adapted to suit circumstances.	✗ Fixed rules about what you 'should' do, or what's 'wrong', 'right', 'good' or 'bad'.
✓ A reflection of the type of person you want to be and the qualities you appreciate in yourself and others.	✗ Always easy to follow and can involve making difficult choices or experiencing uncomfortable feelings.
✓ Personal and may be similar, overlapping or completely different from the people around you.	✗ Chosen to fit in with other people's values or to ignore your own beliefs and opinions.

 Pause and Think **5 Minutes**

Talk about your Guide

Just talking about your Guide and your values can help you find a sense of purpose and improve your mood and wellbeing. Who could you choose to chat with about your values or what matters most to you? It could be someone in your family, a friend or someone else you trust such as a teacher or youth leader. You could show them this exercise and your list of values and use this to get the conversation started. Try asking what their values are and discover how they may be similar or different to yours.

Make a note of what you discover here:

. . . .

. . . .

. . . .

. . . .

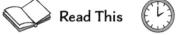 Read This  10 Minutes

Living your values

A value is a general life direction rather than a specific goal or target. You can't tick values such as 'independence', 'variety' or 'fun' off your to-do list, but you can plan and carry out actions that are linked to each of these values. If your value is to learn and grow, then a goal might be to read a book, pass an exam or discover how to fix a car engine. For a value like creativity, your goal might be to paint or draw a picture, make some music or write a story in your journal. Living your values can help to boost your energy, lift your spirits and help you feel more contented and fulfilled.

So, now that you have met your Guide, the next step is to plan some 'towards actions' that move you in the direction of an important value. It's important to make sure these steps are really small and easy to achieve and do not trigger high levels of anxiety or overwhelm.

Taking a towards action often involves getting past some discomfort. For example, if your value is for activity you might choose to go for a bike ride. Getting out on your bike may involve getting past feelings of anxiety or fear about what might happen, as well as other difficult feelings such as tiredness, sadness or boredom. You might also have to pull yourself away from other activities such as zoning out in front of the TV.

'Away actions' are the opposite – they move you away from the things you care about. Examples include not going out to meet a friend you care about because you feel too worried or anxious, or not getting an important task done because you keep worrying about something else.

 Do This 10 Minutes

Take a towards step

In Chapter 12 we will look in more detail at setting goals and planning actions that overcome your anxiety in small steps. For now, can you think of just one *tiny* action that would move you towards an important value? It should take no longer than a few minutes.

Remember, your goal is to take a tiny step towards something you care about. It doesn't matter how small this is! It's more important to pick something easy to achieve, and you can build on this over time.

Write it here:

....

....

....

> **Meera:** Even though I still felt anxious, I decided to take one small step towards one of my values. I'm finding it hard to get out much because of anxiety, so I picked a value that I can do at home: creativity. I used to love being creative in lots of different ways and I haven't done much lately. I found it hard to pick a towards action at first, but in the end, I chose something quick and easy to do. I have always enjoyed nail art – creating different colours and patterns on my nails is fun and makes them look nice. I decided to paint my nails as I still have lots of nail polish in the cupboard at home. I'm not sure if it will help much, but I will give it a go and see what happens.

Pause and Think 5 Minutes

Balancing your values

Take another look at the 4–6 most important values that you chose on pages 133–135. Write them down here:

....

....

....

....

. . . .

. . . .

Now answer these questions:

Are your values balanced, such as including both responsibility and fun?

. . . .

. . . .

. . . .

Have you forgotten, overlooked or ignored any important values recently? How might you start to bring them back into your life?

. . . .

. . . .

. . . .

Are any values becoming overwhelming, demanding, holding you back or limiting you in some way? Can you balance them with other important values?

. . . .

. . . .

. . . .

Are your values clashing?

Sometimes it can feel like your different values are clashing or competing with each other. You might value learning or achievement and set yourself a goal to pass an important exam. Each evening you will need to decide how to use your time. Should you study? Get some exercise? Eat a healthy meal? Go out with your friends? Or take time to relax and sleep?

Making these decisions will depend on lots of things: How soon is the exam? How hungry or tired are you? Will exercise help you focus and concentrate? How much studying have you done already this week? It will also involve thinking about other values such as activity, connection and fun.

The aim is to find a helpful balance between living out your different values. This might take several days, weeks or even months to achieve, but if a value is important, it's best not to ignore it altogether. There is no 'correct' or 'perfect' answer – it's usually a question of trying things out to see what happens and being prepared to change your plans if you need to. And sometimes you can satisfy more than one value at once – such as going for a walk in the park (outdoors/active) and chatting to a friend on the phone at the same time (connection), or listening to a podcast about a subject that interests you (learning).

It's also important to update your values and the direction that your Guide is pointing as your interests and priorities will change as you grow and develop through life. Remember to come back to this chapter regularly and notice how your values are developing over time.

> **Meera:** I spend a lot of time worrying about my schoolwork and my future and this gets in the way of some of my values such as being able to relax and have fun. I've also been quite cut off from my friends – I haven't seen my best friend for ages and we used to hang out all the time. I can see that I've just lost touch with a lot of my values and that makes me feel quite sad. I've decided to message my friend and invite her to my house. I think that would work for two values – fun and connection. I feel nervous, but she's always been very kind as well as lots of fun, so it would be nice to see her. I'm going to give it a try!

 **Read This**    **10 Minutes**

Look for meaning and purpose

Many people say they want to be 'happy', yet strangely enough, trying too hard to find happiness can leave you feeling stressed, frustrated and even more anxious. You might start focusing too much on yourself, judging and criticizing your achievements, constantly trying to satisfy your wants and needs, and comparing yourself negatively to other people.

It's often more rewarding to look for purpose and meaning. This involves looking outwards, finding ways to make a difference in the world and getting involved with things that are bigger than you are. By giving to the wider community, you may find more satisfaction and contentment, feel more optimistic and become better able to cope with problems when things go wrong.

It can also help to seek out others who share your values – to find a tribe of people who understand your point of view. Finding just one other person who shares a value might be enough, or you may find a whole community to offer encouragement. This could be face-to-face or via an online or virtual group.

 Do This   10 Minutes

Finding your own sense of purpose

Look at this list of ways to increase your sense of meaning and purpose in life. Which ones could you try?

Ideas for finding meaning and purpose	Examples	What could you try?
Connect with others, finding ways to share your hopes, fears, successes and failures.	Talk to an understanding friend or supportive adult about the things that are most important to you, or listen to someone else who is struggling.	
Give some time to your local community.	Find a way to volunteer your time and get involved. Could you support your local parkrun, Scouts or Brownies, or a local community youth group?	
Step up to a new challenge and develop new skills and experiences.	Sign up for a leadership position at school or college or learn a new skill that can benefit others, such as first aid.	
Get involved in a cause that you care about.	Find ways to make your family or school greener, join a life-saving club or a local environmental group, or call out discrimination when you see it.	
Find ways to explore the world around you.	Join a new club or activity, apply for a part-time job, learn a new language or explore your local area with friends.	

 **Read This** **10 Minutes**

Follow your Guide... even when you feel anxious!
Thinking about your values and following your Guide is extra important when you are feeling anxious. If anxiety makes you avoid or cut down on many things that matter to you, you may also start to feel fed up, low or depressed. To prevent this, it's important to keep following your Guide, doing things you know are important, knowing that this can increase your confidence and improve how you feel. You could think of this as surfing a wave and staying on your board, feeling the thrill of riding over it. Or riding your bike over a bump in the road and continuing to stay on track, doing what matters.

 Pause and Think **5 Minutes**

Following your Guide through discomfort
Think of a time when you felt apprehensive or nervous about doing something but did it anyway because it was important. You could choose a time that you spoke up for someone, completed a sports challenge, took an exam or went into a new situation.

Describe the situation. What happened? What did you do?	
What uncomfortable thoughts and feelings did you overcome to do this?	
What were your important values? Were you following your Guide?	
What was the long-term effect of overcoming these difficult thoughts and feelings?	

Summary: using your Guide

→ Your Guide points towards the things in life that matter most to you.

→ Following your Guide involves asking yourself questions such as 'Who and what do I care about?' and 'What kind of person do I want to be?'

→ Living your values involves planning 'towards actions' which move you in the direction of an important value, even if these involve overcoming challenges or feel hard at first.

→ Your goal is to find a balance between different values and to stop anxiety from getting in the way of your important values.

Final thoughts

Make a note of anything you have found helpful, interesting or surprising from this chapter.

....

....

....

....

....

....

What are you going to do now? Can you choose one small action based on what you have discovered from this chapter?

....

....

....

....

....

....

Chapter 12

READY FOR ACTION

Niall: Anxiety holds me back in life. Sometimes I feel too anxious to go anywhere, so I end up making excuses not to go out or meet friends. At other times, I get stuck in my head, with worries going round and round and it feels impossible to think straight or get anything done. All this constant anxiety takes so much time and energy that I often can't be bothered to do many things I used to enjoy. I know I miss out on opportunities because of my anxiety, and this makes me feel fed up and even more anxious about the future.

When you are feeling anxious or worried, you can get stuck in a pattern of anxiety actions, such as avoiding situations that might make you anxious, putting things off or trying to distract yourself from anxiety using technology, alcohol or drugs. Although they may seem to work initially, these types of actions can all give anxiety a 'super-boost' and make it grow stronger over time. Missing out on enjoyable and exciting experiences and opportunities can also make you feel fed up and stuck, and it can start to feel like anxiety is controlling your life.

The good news is that it's possible to change this negative pattern. Even small increases in your daily activities can build your confidence, lift your mood and energy, give you a greater sense of achievement and enjoyment from life and help you to feel more connected to your friends and family.

We are going to explore how to get Ready for Action.

This builds on Chapter 11, where you met your Guide and started to think about what things are important to you. Being Ready for Action is a simple but effective way of taking back control of your life and stopping anxiety from limiting your choices and possibilities. So, in this chapter we will learn how to:

→ do more things that are important, enjoyable or meaningful, even if you are also dealing with anxiety, worry thoughts, difficult feelings and stressful life events

→ choose actions that can boost your confidence and energy, lift your mood and increase your energy and enthusiasm

→ plan realistic small changes or 'micro-steps' that are easy to achieve

→ move up the Confidence Ladder, coming out of the Safety Zone and into the Stretch and Growth Zones.

 **Read This** **10 Minutes**

 ## Follow your Guide and do what matters

In this chapter, we are going to explore ways to do more things that matter to you and make life feel more exciting, interesting and filled with adventure. This can be exciting and fulfilling but may also lead to feelings of anxiety. The Anxiety Train passengers may start to show up with their negative stories of doom and catastrophe. However, you don't need to let these scaremongers stop you from doing what's important. We will explore many ways to cope with anxious thoughts and worries in Chapter 14.

You might also experience body sensations that can be uncomfortable or scary. Remember, these feelings are unpleasant but not dangerous, and will always pass with time. If you start to notice these sensations when trying something new, you could try using the 54321 technique that we learned in Chapter 6. We will also learn many new skills for coping with unpleasant feelings of anxiety in Chapter 13.

 Pause and Think **10 Minutes**

Which activities are important to you?

Following your Guide often involves starting to face your fears as you embrace new situations and experiences. This can be scary at first, but it is often worth the effort as you take control of your life and feel more able to do the things that matter to you.

Take a few minutes to think about what kinds of activities are important, enjoyable or meaningful to you. Use the following questions to help you think about your Guide and how this might affect which actions and activities you choose.

Who and what is most important to you? In what direction does your Guide point? Turn back to Chapter 11 for a reminder if you need to.	
What activities did you enjoy or do regularly in the past? Is there anything that you would like to get involved with again?	
What kinds of activities might move you towards your important values, both now and in the future? Be creative and think as widely as you can.	
Imagine you could wave a magic wand and feel energetic, enthusiastic and happy. How would this affect how you spent your day? What would you do?	

Here are Niall's answers.

Who and what is most important to you? What direction does your Guide point in?	*I'm really into music – I like listening to my favourite bands and I also play the guitar. My friends are important to me, but I get nervous in social situations, so I tend not to see them outside of college. I'd like to feel I fit in better and have fun with my mates more often.*
What activities did you enjoy or do regularly in the past? Is there anything that you would like to get involved with again?	*I used to swim three times a week in a swimming club, but since I gave that up a few years ago, I don't do much exercise or sport. I'd like to be fitter and more active again.*
What kinds of activities might move you towards your important values, both now and in the future? Be creative and think as widely as you can.	*I'd love to play in a band, and also to watch more live music. I would also do more exercise, maybe swimming once a week or I could do something related to swimming like training to be a lifeguard.*
Imagine you could wave a magic wand and feel energetic, enthusiastic and happy. How would this affect how you spent your day? What would you do?	*I would go to college and be less worried about what I'm going to say, so I'd be able to chat and make jokes with my friends. I might ask them to hang out in the evening. I might also go to the music department and find out how I could start playing music with other people.*

Read This **10 Minutes**

Change your actions with 'micro-steps'

One of the best ways to start getting Ready for Action is to make changes really small and achievable using 'micro-steps'. These are tiny changes that are realistic and easy to achieve. Each micro-step takes only a few minutes to complete and does not involve anything too scary or overwhelming.

Using micro-steps can help you to build your confidence by achieving lots of small successes. You can behave 'as if...' you feel slightly more confident and just a little less anxious. Choosing to take micro-steps can help you learn that you don't need to feel stuck and powerless in the face of anxiety. Instead, you can have a choice to take control of your actions. Each small success will build your confidence and make it easier to do a little more next time.

At first, you might still feel quite anxious. The Anxiety Train passengers may show up and tell you that this won't help or that something terrible could go wrong. But... you can take small steps anyway and see what happens. What's important is not whether you feel anxious but whether you have been able to get Ready for Action, no matter how small this action might be!

Do This **10 Minutes**

Plan your own micro-steps

Look at the box below with some examples of micro-steps. Pick two or three ideas. Can you commit to carrying these out within the next few days? Remember, each one should take only a few minutes to complete.

When planning a micro-step, remember to ask yourself:

→ **What** are you planning to try?

→ **When** and **where** will you try it?

→ **Who** or what can help you achieve this step?

→ **What skills** can you use to help you successfully cope with any difficulties or challenges?

→ **How confident** are you that you can achieve this? Do you need to make your goal smaller or easier, or ask for some support to complete it?

Examples of micro-steps	What are your ideas?
Message a friend to see how they are.	
Make a healthy snack.	
Look up what's on at the cinema.	
Find your trainers and put them by the front door.	
Dance to a song you like.	
Go for a 5-minute walk around the block.	
Look up a new recipe to try.	
Practice five basketball shots in the garden.	

Niall: I've always enjoyed music and playing the guitar but lately I've been feeling fed up and haven't picked it up for ages. I decided that I would get my guitar back into tune and then play one song. I felt frustrated at first because I'd forgotten something I used to play easily, but I took a breath and kept going. After a few tries it started to come back again. I enjoyed playing and I will try to play for a few minutes each day. It's a great way for me to relax and wind down after a busy day.

 Read This 10 Minutes

Build your confidence to do important activities

One way to build your confidence to do important activities without becoming over-whelmed or panicky is to start to challenge yourself to do things that are just outside your normal Safety Zone. Let's look at the different confidence zones:

Safety Zone	Life in the Safety Zone feels very safe and secure and there are few challenges! It is good for resting and relaxing, but if you spend too long there you can miss out on important opportunities. Being stuck in a Safety Zone rut involves restricting your life and only choosing activities that you can already do with little thought or effort. This can be quite boring and over time can shrink your confidence and increase your anxiety.

Stretch Zone	As you take small steps outside the Safety Zone, you move into the Stretch Zone. Here, you are starting to take a few small risks and try some new things. You are more willing to experiment with life, discover what happens when you make changes and learn from your experiences. As you move into the Stretch Zone, you may find that life starts to change and new possibilities begin to open up. Your confidence begins to grow as you recognize that you are capable of rising to new challenges.
Growth Zone	In the Growth Zone, you are fully committed to trying new things, learning new skills and developing new abilities as you work towards important goals. Your confidence remains high in your ability to learn and adapt to challenges. You are also using your ability to bounce back from setbacks or obstacles. You can draw on your inner confidence to keep going by looking for solutions and finding new pathways to successful outcomes. The Growth Zone is where you start to get skilful at what you choose to do.
Overload Zone	In the Overload Zone, you have taken on a challenge that feels a little too overwhelming or difficult. If this happens, your confidence can take a dip, you may start to feel stressed and anxious and your performance might drop. It's wise to try to avoid reaching the Overload Zone when setting challenges and goals to maximize your chances of success and to keep your confidence high. However, if you do reach this point, it's not a disaster. Simply recognize what has happened and drop back down into the Growth Zone or Stretch Zone. You don't have to retreat to the Safety Zone as this can get in the way of making progress towards your goals.

 Read This   10 Minutes

Stepping outside of the Safety Zone

You don't have to take a giant leap from one zone to the next. Think about taking a small step outside the zone you are currently in.

You can do this, even if you have feelings of anxiety, self-doubt or uncertainty. By behaving 'as if' you feel a little less anxious, you may find that you start to feel more confident too. And even if your feelings don't change, by acting with more confidence you are more likely to achieve things that matter to you.

Acting with confidence involves:

→ putting in time and effort to develop your skills and knowledge to achieve goals or take part in activities that you care about or want to improve in

→ trying new experiences and new ways of doing things

→ taking part in challenges such as tests, performances and competitions

→ communicating with confidence using both words and body language

→ learning and developing based on constructive feedback

→ problem-solving and using your inner skills and strengths to handle problems or obstacles.

There are many ways to stretch yourself outside the Safety Zone to build your confidence and overcome anxiety! Can you challenge yourself to take a really small step into the Stretch Zone by picking something that's just beyond what you might normally choose? You might decide to volunteer for a new project, sign up for a committee, try out for a team or a talent show, raise your hand and ask more questions or take a risk and talk to someone new.

Be kind to yourself, as taking the first step may be difficult or scary. To help motivate you, follow your Guide and pick something that you genuinely care about. Look at this list of activities, which might give you some ideas.

Ways to stretch your confidence	Examples of confidence stretching in action	What might *you* try?
Stretching or improving one of your existing skills	*I like tennis and I'd like to try playing with someone new.* *I love cooking and I'd like to try a new recipe.*	I will…
Learning or developing a new skill	*I've never done public speaking before…I could join an acting group or a debating club.*	I will…
Expressing your own ideas and opinions	*I'm going to share my love of reading by joining a book club and telling others my views on a particular book.* *I'm going to put my hand up and answer questions more in my study group.*	I will…
Trying new hobbies and interests	*I've always wanted to learn about coding, photography, car engines, singing…I'm going to join an online course or a local group.*	I will…
Taking the lead by organizing or running things	*I'm going to stand for class representative or volunteer to take the lead in making a change at my workplace.*	I will…

cont.

Ways to stretch your confidence	Examples of confidence stretching in action	What might *you* try?
Feeling more in control by planning, tidying and organizing	*I will organize my bedroom or my wardrobe the way I like it. I will plan my schedule to make sure I can fit in all the things that are important to me. I'll keep an eye on my finances so I can save up for something that I want.*	I will...
Using your knowledge	*I know about plants, sports, DIY, fixing things...I will take on a bigger project, learn something new or find a way to share my knowledge with others.*	I will...

Once you have taken your first small step into the Stretch Zone, pick something else to try. Do you want to build on this activity or try something completely different? Keep repeating this process. Confidence grows with every step forward.

> **Niall:** I decided to use my interest in music to help me talk to someone in my class who I've seen carrying a guitar around the campus. At the end of class, I said 'hi' and asked what kind of guitar he played. He was keen to talk to me about it and we ended up sitting together at lunch. It turns out he likes a lot of the same bands that I do. I usually sit by myself, so it felt good to have company and I felt more confident afterwards. I will definitely chat with him again!

Use SPICE to balance your activities

Sometimes it can be helpful to expand the range of things you do to increase motivation and reduce boredom. To do this, you can add some **SPICE** to your day or week! This means completing activities that involve one of the following:

→ **S**uccess or achievement

→ **P**hysical activity and moving your body

→ **I**mportant or meaningful

→ **C**onnection or closeness to others

→ **E**njoyable, relaxing and fun.

The following table includes examples of many different types of SPICE activities that can give more ideas about how to climb up the Confidence Ladder and do more enjoyable and interesting activities. Put a tick against any you might try, and add your own ideas and interests to the list.

Type of activity	Examples	What are your ideas? How can you climb the Confidence Ladder?
Success or achievement	Try a new recipe or an old favourite. Learn something new. Sign up for an acting class. Build a website or write a blog. Finish a project you've been putting off. Rearrange your bedroom. Write a poem, rap or short story. Tick something off your to-do list.	
Physical activity	Go jogging, running or for a bike ride. Go for a swim or to the gym. Jump on a skateboard or roller skates. Bounce on the trampoline. Dance to a song. Practise football, tennis or basketball. Do an online workout. Mow the lawn or do some gardening.	
Important or meaningful	Volunteer for a local charity. Take your driving test or learn first aid. Watch an online lesson. Learn to repair your bike. Apply for work experience or a job. Campaign for a change in the world. Go to the dentist.	
Connection or closeness	Invite friends for a movie night. Cuddle your pet. Message or FaceTime someone. Play a board game. Make a card for a friend or grandparent. Go window shopping with someone. Look at photos of your favourite people.	

cont.

Type of activity	Examples	What are your ideas? How can you climb the Confidence Ladder?
Enjoyable, relaxing or fun	Play an instrument or listen to music. Watch a comedy or a funny video. Do a jigsaw, craft activity or construct something with Lego. Put on makeup or your favourite outfit. Take a long shower or a bubble bath.	

 Read This  5 Minutes

Create a routine

One way to get more active is to make it part of your daily routine. You can start by keeping a record of your activity levels using your phone, diary or planner. This will help you to keep track of your achievements and can motivate you to continue making changes and setting yourself new challenges. And as your new patterns of activity turn into habits, it becomes easier to keep doing them.

Take some time each week to look through your diary and check how you are getting on. This will help to keep you on the right track. Make sure your routine is flexible and can adapt to any new situations or events.

 Do This  10 Minutes Per Day

Use an activity diary

Can you practise keeping track of your daily activities over the next few weeks using the diary template below or noting it on your phone? Notice whether they are SPICE activities. What effect did the activity have on your mood – how did you feel after doing it?

Day			What was the activity? How long did you do it?	Was it a SPICE activity? Success or achievement Physical activity Important or meaningful Connection or closeness Enjoyment or fun	Which confidence zone were you in? (Safety, Stretch, Growth or Overload?)
Monday	Morning				
	Afternoon				
	Evening				
Tuesday	Morning				
	Afternoon				
	Evening				
Wednesday	Morning				
	Afternoon				
	Evening				
Thursday	Morning				
	Afternoon				
	Evening				
Friday	Morning				
	Afternoon				
	Evening				
Saturday	Morning				
	Afternoon				
	Evening				
Sunday	Morning				
	Afternoon				
	Evening				

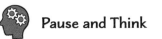 **Pause and Think**  **10 Minutes**

Swap anxiety actions for positive actions

As we learned in Chapter 3, anxiety can have a big effect on your actions. You retreat into the Safety Zone and stop doing many enjoyable and important activities. So far, we've focused on increasing these activities in small steps outside of the zone.

Alongside this, it's also helpful to cut down on any unhelpful anxiety actions. Look at the following list. Which anxiety actions can you recognize? How can you start to swap these actions for more positive ones that move you towards your Guide and the things you care about? Can you find ways to challenge yourself to move up the Confidence Ladder?

Type of anxiety action	Example of swapping this	What could you try?
Avoiding what makes you anxious, even if it's important	*I could try going with someone else the first time.*	
Checking and double-checking, such as looking online or checking your body	*I'll just check once and then I'll get on with my day. I won't spend longer than 5 minutes looking online.*	
Put off starting something important because you feel anxious about what will happen	*I will plan to do the first 5 minutes of the project to get myself started.*	
Spending lots of time worrying and focusing on what might go wrong, rather than doing things that matter to you	*If I notice I'm worrying I will get up and dance to a song or call my friend.*	

Spending so much time planning or preparing for something that you don't get around to doing other important things	*I'll set myself an alarm for 30 minutes of planning time and then stop!*	
Repeatedly asking others for reassurance that you are safe or that problems won't happen	*I'll ask just once and write down what they say to help me remember it when I'm feeling anxious.*	

Niall: I find it hard to do my coursework because I feel anxious and stressed about getting it right. I keep thinking it might not go well or I might make a mistake. This means it can take a long time to do things – even a short piece of work can take hours to finish because I put off getting started. This week, I decided to do the first five minutes of my homework straight after getting home. I stepped into the Stretch Zone and decided to just have a go and see what happens rather than waiting to feel completely sure. It felt weird at first and quite uncomfortable, but it did feel good that it wasn't hanging over me all evening. I read back over my work afterwards and it wasn't that bad! I'm going to try and keep this up because I finished my work a lot earlier than usual, so I had more time to relax and play my guitar afterwards.

Summary: get Ready for Action!

→ Getting Ready for Action involves doing more things that are important, enjoyable or meaningful.

→ 'Micro-steps' can help to build your confidence as you achieve many small successes.

→ Challenge yourself to take small steps out of the Safety Zone and into the Stretch and the Growth Zones.

→ Swap out your unhelpful anxiety actions for more positive and helpful SPICE activities that follow your Guide.

Final thoughts

Make a note of anything you have found helpful, interesting or surprising from this chapter.

....

....

....

....

....

....

What are you going to do now? Can you choose one small action based on what you have discovered?

....

....

....

....

....

....

Chapter 13

OPEN AND OBSERVE

Imogen: When I'm anxious, I find it really hard to focus and my mind feels like it's all over the place. I'm constantly thinking about everything that might go wrong, or worrying about something that I did or said the day before. It can make it difficult to pay attention to things, and I find it hard to watch a TV programme without my mind drifting away so I miss out on what's happening. The same thing happens in lessons at school. I'm often so busy worrying that I don't hear what the teacher has said.

Learning to Open and Observe involves paying attention to what's going on inside you and in the world around you. This is a useful skill that can help you focus on important things in the here and now, rather than getting distracted by thoughts, worries or uncomfortable feelings of anxiety.

In this chapter, we will explore how you can learn to:

➜ recognize what's happening in your body and mind and the world around you

➜ notice your thoughts without believing all the scary stories that the Anxiety Train passengers may bring into your mind

➜ learn to cope with uncomfortable feelings of anxiety without getting overwhelmed

➜ find ways to get more involved and find greater enjoyment from your daily activities.

Pause and Think **10 Minutes**

Do you get stuck in your head?

When you are feeling anxious, it's easy to get trapped in your mind, listening to the negative stories of the Anxiety Train passengers such as Scaremonger, Worry-Worm, Panic Button Pusher or Confidence-Crusher.

They always think the worst and focus on everything that might go wrong, predicting future potential disasters and telling you that you can't cope with even small problems. These anxious thoughts can go around endlessly, like a broken record, making it difficult to concentrate on your activities or to motivate yourself to do things, even if they are important.

Do you ever get trapped in negative thoughts and worries? Which Anxiety Train passengers are most likely to show up in your mind?	
Can you think of an example of when worrying about problems has stopped you from concentrating or focusing on an important task?	
What was the impact of this? What problems happened as a result?	

 Read This **10 Minutes**

How can Open and Observe help?

Using Open and Observe involves developing skills in mindfulness where you start to be more aware of what's happening in your body and mind. This can help you to break free from anxious thoughts and feelings. It also helps you to pay attention to whatever's important in the here and now and creates chances for you to notice and appreciate more positive or enjoyable parts of your life.

No matter how distressing they are, it's impossible to just 'get rid of' anxious thoughts and feelings. Using Open and Observe is not about trying to make your mind go blank or trying to get rid of these completely. Instead, you can step back and notice that the uncomfortable thought or feeling has shown up and then give it some space to pass in its own time rather than fighting to get rid of it. Doing this means that even though the difficult thoughts and feelings may stay for a while, they will be easier to cope with and have less effect on how you live your life.

 **Do This**  **30 Seconds**

Notice your feet
It's easy to forget we even have feet, but they are there waiting for you to notice them! Bring your attention to your feet. Wriggle your toes and lift your heels, pressing the balls of your feet into the ground. Now rock back onto your heels and notice the stretch at the back of your calf. Repeat this movement two or three times.

What sensations did you notice in your feet and legs?	
Did any thoughts show up in your mind? Did you notice any feelings or emotions?	

Congratulations! You were *Open* to physical sensations, thoughts and feelings and *Observed* them for 30 seconds.

 **Read This** **10 Minutes**

Strengthen your attention muscle
To build Open and Observe skills, it's helpful to practise regularly, ideally every day. You can think of this as strengthening your attention muscle. It will grow stronger each

time you use it. This doesn't have to take a lot of time. Just a few minutes, or even a few seconds, each day can help you start to become more aware and better able to cope with difficult thoughts and feelings.

Here are some different short activities that will help to strengthen your attention muscle and build Open and Observe skills.

 **Do This**  **2-10 Minutes**

Pay attention to daily activities

Practise doing an everyday activity, such as taking a shower or brushing your teeth, with a little more focus and awareness. This might even help turn a routine or boring activity into something that gives you a little more satisfaction or creates a sense of calm. It helps if you use different senses – sight, taste, smell, touch and hearing. Experiment with some of the following suggestions.

Ways to use Open and Observe skills	What could you do?	Where and when could you try this?
During a shower or bath	Notice the warmth and refreshing flow of water and breathe in the smell of your favourite shampoo or shower gel.	
Brushing your teeth	Listen to the sounds and notice the sensations and minty taste as you brush around each tooth and your gums.	
Being active or moving your body	Observe your body moving during an activity or exercise. Can you notice the feel of your feet on the ground, your legs moving and the sensation in different muscles as you stretch your arms above your head or gently touch your toes?	

Talking to someone	Focus on the person you are talking to. Notice the sound of their voice and the words they are saying. Can you say something that shows you have been listening?	
Eating and drinking	Pay attention when you are eating or drinking. Can you notice the smell, temperature and texture? Pause before swallowing and feel the sensations as the food or drink moves down your throat.	
Any other regular daily activity	Choose something else that you do each day to pay attention to. Use all your senses: vision, hearing, touch, taste and smell.	

 Pause and Think  **5 Minutes**

Pick one or more examples or choose your own. Can you commit to trying this at least three to five times a week for two weeks?	
How could you remember to do this? Can you set an alarm on your phone or leave a Post-it note in the bathroom as a reminder?	
After you've practised for a while, what can you notice? What's the effect of this activity?	

Do This   **3–10 Minutes**

Here are some more ways that you could practise focusing on what you are doing in the present moment. Each of these activities need only take around 3–10 minutes to complete.

Mindful walking

Take a short walk, outside or inside, using your senses to be more aware as you move your body. As you walk, take time to look at your surroundings. What colours or shapes are there? Can you notice something you haven't seen before?

What sounds can you notice? Can you hear the sound of your footsteps as you walk, the rustling of your clothes, the breeze in your ears or your breath? Can you smell or taste anything?

What can you feel or touch? Notice the sensation of your feet in contact with the ground. Try taking a few extra slow steps, gradually shifting your weight as you move and noticing the many small sensations in your feet and legs.

When you find yourself getting distracted or your mind drifting away, simply bring your attention back to noticing the physical sensations of walking.

Focus on listening

Take a few minutes to focus on one or more sounds. You could play a favourite piece of music or open the window and listen to the sounds outside.

Close your eyes and notice what sounds you can hear. What's the loudest sound? How about the quietest?

If you are listening to music, pay attention to the different instruments and vocals and how these change through the song. If you have heard the music before, can you notice anything new about it? Try counting how often a particular sound or lyric repeats itself through the track.

Remain as focused as you can for just one song. If you find your mind wandering, congratulate yourself for noticing and then bring your attention back to the music.

Mindful breathing

Sit comfortably with your eyes closed or look down at the ground in front of you. Breathe in and then allow a long sigh as you breathe out slowly. Let your body settle and start to feel heavier.

Notice your breathing. You might be able to feel air moving through your nostrils, across your upper lip or at the back of your throat. Maybe you can feel the rise and fall of your chest or the gentle movement of your belly up and down with each breath.

Gently focus on one area of your body where you can notice your breathing. Notice each breath in and each breath out and perhaps the short pause in between.

Can you bring a friendly attitude to this practice? You could try wishing yourself well in dealing with all the challenges that life brings.

When you find your mind wandering, as it will sometimes, just gently bring it back to the next breath with kindness and patience. Each time you notice that your mind has drifted is a moment of attention and awareness.

> **Imogen:** My mind wanders all over the place so I decided to practise a few minutes of Open and Observe each day to help me learn to get more focused. I like to listen to music, so I decided to listen to one song on the way to school each morning. I put on my headphones and listened closely to the music and the lyrics. I also tried to practise using my five senses for a few minutes by noticing the colours, smells and sounds on the journey. I felt more settled and calmer when I got to school and more ready to learn. If I get lost in thoughts or worries when someone is talking, I also try to use my senses to pay attention – I try to hear and see them. That helps me to concentrate more on what they are saying.

Finding your flow

When you are in a state of 'flow' you are completely absorbed and focused on a task or activity. You let go of thoughts, worries or regrets about the past or future and focus on the here and now. Time flies by as you forget about everything but what you are doing at that moment.

Finding your flow often brings feelings of contentment and satisfaction in whatever you are doing. You can find this in many different ways: as you participate in a physical activity or sport, complete something creative, do a project or write an essay, or even during routine daily tasks.

Have you ever felt fully captured by a great book with an exciting storyline? Have you felt completely absorbed as you played a sport or activity? Have you ever had so much fun with a group of friends that the time just flew by? Have you ever felt transfixed by a beautiful sunrise or by a piece of music that completely captures your attention? These all involve finding your flow.

Pause and Think **5 Minutes**

Can you think of a time that you were fully absorbed or engaged in an activity? What was this?	
What helped you stay focused? How did it feel to be totally absorbed?	

 Do This **2–10 Minutes**

Practise finding your Flow

It's often easier to be absorbed when you are doing something that you find interesting or enjoyable. Therefore, it's worth making sure that you include some of these activities in your daily routine.

Think about the activities you wrote down in the exercise above. What draws you in and holds your interest or attention? It could involve painting, drawing, singing, playing a sport or even doing a chore that you find calming or soothing.

Try bringing your full attention to this activity for just a few minutes. This might help you find your flow as you get completely absorbed without thinking about distractions. It may be tricky at first, but with regular practice, it's easy to build your focus. Start with a few minutes and then build up the time. Using your five senses to notice what you can see, feel, hear, taste and smell as you carry out the activity will help you to focus on it.

 **Read This** **5 Minutes**

Flexing your attention

Imogen: Once I start worrying, it's really hard to stop, and sometimes it escalates until I'm feeling scared or panicky. I try to tell myself to stop worrying but it doesn't seem to help. The thoughts just keep going round and round my head. It can take up a lot of time and makes me feel fed up.

Open and Observe can help if you are stuck in anxious thoughts and worries. If you are feeling panicky, you can also try 54321, which we introduced in Chapter 6.

You can also learn to 'flex your attention'. This involves keeping your mind open and flexible, rather than getting stuck or 'hooked' by anxious thoughts or worries. You can practise this by noticing what's happening around you, then looking inwards to observe your inner thoughts or feelings, and then shifting back out to your surroundings again as you decide what to do next.

Learning to flex your attention can help you to act in ways that are helpful and follow your Guide as you stay in touch with your important values. This is similar to Noticing the NOW, which we introduced in Chapter 1.

 **Do This**   **2–5 Minutes**

Practise flexing your attention

Practise this attention-flexing exercise for a few minutes daily if you tend to get stuck in worry thoughts.

→ Notice a sensation in your body – it may help to exaggerate this by moving your body a little. Push your feet onto the floor, scrunch your toes or stretch your arms up above your head. Pause for 10–20 seconds and notice the feel of your body.

→ Now move your attention to a sound. It might be something you can hear in your environment, or you can create a sound by gently humming or tapping on the desk. Pause for 10–20 seconds and notice the sound.

→ Shift your attention to something that you can see nearby. Take 10–20 seconds to really look at this, noticing the object's colours, shape, shadows and textures.

→ Now flex again and shift to what's happening inside you. Take 10–20 seconds to notice what thoughts and feelings are happening right now. Can you name an emotion? Or a body sensation? Is there anything that you have an urge to act on, such as hunger, thirst, an itch or stiffness?

→ Finally, can you widen your attention to notice several different things at the same time? This might include physical sensations, sounds, thoughts, emotions or what you can see.

After carrying out attention shifting, take a minute to pause and think. What have you discovered? What's the most important thing to focus on next in your day?

Imogen: Flexing my attention has helped me a lot when I am stuck worrying or with thoughts going round and round in my head without getting anywhere. I practised noticing sounds around me, then things I can see and finally sensations in my body. When I came back to what was important, I realized I felt less anxious and it was easier to get on with doing something positive. I've tried to combine this with the skills I learned in the chapter on getting Ready for Action. I found that this has helped me do a lot more things that I care about.

 Read This **2 Minutes**

Noticing happiness or enjoyment

You can also use Open and Observe skills to get better at noticing even tiny moments of happiness or contentment in your day.

Your brain is programmed to look out for risky, scary or negative events to try to avoid danger and keep you safe. This is a survival instinct, but it also means that you can often overlook some of the more enjoyable parts of life.

Instead, why not take a few minutes to think about some of the things that you appreciate and enjoy? This isn't about ignoring or shutting out problems but involves deliberately taking time to observe and appreciate any small moment that's enjoyable alongside things that make you feel anxious or fed up. It's like shining a torch on something colourful, beautiful or interesting on a dark damp night, which can help you feel calmer, safer and happier.

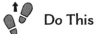 **Do This**   **5 Minutes**

Appreciate something small...

Take 5 minutes to notice and enjoy small things in your day that you can appreciate, using some of your senses. Describe them to yourself as you take it all in:

→ *I see...* What things do you appreciate visually or enjoy looking at? It might be a flower in your garden, looking out to sea, someone's face or a building with an interesting shape. Notice any colours, shapes and patterns. Take a slow breath and allow yourself to appreciate that you can experience the amazing world of colour and shape.

→ *I smell... I taste...* Have you enjoyed eating or drinking anything today? Imagine the flavour and texture and breathe in the smell deeply. Think about all the people who have been involved in growing the ingredients, harvesting, transporting and selling them so they can reach you. Can you send them a little thanks and appreciation for their effort and hard work?

→ *I can touch and feel...* What do you like to hold or feel? Maybe it's the gentle pressure of water in a shower or bath, a pet you love to stroke, a soft material that feels warm and calming, or hugging someone. You could try stroking your arm from the shoulder down to the hand. Or place a hand over your heart, noticing the warmth and the pressure and wish yourself well. Give yourself a quick moment of thanks and appreciation for all the effort and hard work you do each day.

> **Imogen:** This week, I took a few minutes each evening to think about some things that I appreciated or enjoyed during the day, and I wrote them down in my diary. I just picked small things, like enjoying a sandwich at lunchtime or remembering how my friend looked happy when I gave her a birthday card. Yesterday was a lovely sunny day and I enjoyed sitting outside at break time. Even though the things are quite small, it made me feel happy to remember them. I found myself noticing nice things more during the day and planning to write them down in my journal. I definitely plan to keep doing this.

Summary: Open and Observe

➔ Open and Observe involves noticing your inner reactions and the world around you.

➔ You can strengthen your attention muscle by focusing on your everyday activities for just a few minutes each day.

➔ You can improve your focus and get 'in the zone' when doing an activity you enjoy.

➔ Practise flexing your attention if you often become stuck having anxiety thoughts or worries.

➔ You can use Open and Observe to notice small moments of contentment and happiness in your day.

Final thoughts

Make a note of anything you have found helpful, interesting or surprising from this chapter.

....
....
....
....
....
....

What are you going to do now? Can you choose one small action based on what you have discovered?

....
....
....
....
....
....

Chapter 14

WISE MIND

Archie: My mind is constantly coming up with 'what if...?' thoughts about problems and things that might go wrong. I try telling myself to think more positively but the thoughts seem to get stuck in my head and make me anxious and stressed. I don't know how to get rid of them!

I worry about so many different things! Schoolwork and exams, friendships and how I played at football practice... I spend a lot of time going over and over what I said and did, and how I could have done it better, or worrying about the future and whether I will mess it up next time. I wish I could be a bit more relaxed and care less about what other people think of me.

 ## What is Wise Mind?

Your mind is made up of the many thoughts, beliefs, stories and images which help you to make sense of the world around you. It develops and changes throughout your life, and it is shaped by many things, including your personality, family background, people around you and events in your life.

Your mind cannot be seen by other people, but it will affect how you feel and react in the outer world. When you feel anxious or panicky, you may spend a lot of time thinking about possible problems, focusing on worst-case scenarios and exaggerating the risks that something bad may happen. You might also underestimate your ability to cope with difficult situations or assume that you appear worse to others than you do.

Listening to your Wise Mind is very different to believing the scary messages from your Threat system and the passengers of the Anxiety Train. Using Wise Mind involves looking at the big picture, keeping faith in your abilities and thinking flexibly. Wise

Mind offers you a choice so you can look for helpful ways to meet challenges and overcome problems rather than react to Anxiety Train passengers.

In this chapter, we will:

→ practise noticing anxious thoughts without believing everything that the Anxiety Train passengers are saying

→ meet your Wise Mind and discover more balanced and helpful ways of looking at the world

→ learn some new ways to deal with anxious and scary thoughts or worries.

 **Read This** **10 Minutes**

Spot your anxious thoughts

When your Threat system is set off, the Anxiety Train passengers will bring scary thoughts into your mind that are exaggerated and which lead you into spirals of anxiety and panic. The first step in using Wise Mind is to *notice* what's going on in your mind: What thoughts have shown up? What is your mind telling you?

Observing anxious thoughts will not make them disappear but it can make them less powerful. This is like turning down the volume on a scary TV channel so the loud shrieks don't sound so shocking or interfere with living your life.

You can remind yourself that these anxious thoughts are just one point of view and are not concrete facts. Like rainclouds passing across the sky, thoughts will come and go and can change in different situations. You can have a different opinion about the same issue on different days, or you might find out new information and change your mind. When your Anxiety Alarm system is switched on, you will often jump to negative conclusions and assume the worst. But as you learn to switch it off again, you may see things very differently. By paying less attention to anxious thoughts, they will have less impact on your emotions and how you live your life.

 **Do This** **5 Minutes**

Name your thoughts

Next time you are stuck having anxious thoughts or worries, try naming your thoughts. Use one or more of the following phrases to help you notice what's happening in your mind. It may help to write it down in a journal, on a Post-it note or on your phone or computer. You can experiment with changing the size, font and colour and see if this alters how much you believe the thought.

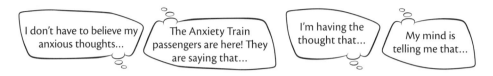

Remember, you don't have to believe everything that the Anxiety Train passengers are telling you! If you pause and wait for a short while, letting your anxiety subside, you might notice that more positive or balanced thoughts also start to appear.

No matter what thoughts show up, you can choose how to react to them. Ask yourself: What's the most helpful thing that you can do next?

 **Read This**   **10 Minutes**

 ## Meet your Wise Mind

Your Wise Mind is like having a best friend or a supportive coach or teacher who motivates you through encouragement, kindness and wisdom, rather than blaming, criticizing or scaring you. Your Wise Mind believes that you can succeed. You can keep looking for solutions to problems and keep going even if things don't work out the first time, or you can let go of unhelpful thoughts that keep you trapped.

You can use Wise Mind to help you make wise choices when you are facing difficult situations. You can't guarantee what will happen in the future, but you can choose how to approach problems and difficult situations. Choosing actions that are helpful and that follow your Guide will often lead to you feeling happier, more in control of life and acting like the person you wish to be.

When you are feeling anxious or uncertain, your Wise Mind:

→ is helpful and encouraging, looking for ways to solve problems

→ has a kind and friendly attitude, even if you have made a mistake or something has gone wrong

→ wants the best for you and others as well

→ reminds you of your strengths and abilities, and that you are capable of dealing with difficult situations

→ encourages you to follow your Guide and do important things, helping you to face new situations and uncertainty in the pursuit of what matters.

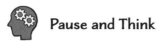 Pause and Think    10 Minutes

Who or what inspires your Wise Mind?

Have you ever known an inspiring teacher, coach, instructor or family member? What were they like? What would they say to you or to others who were struggling? How did they encourage you? Can you keep any of their advice in mind when feeling anxious or when you are facing problems or difficult situations?

Who else inspires you with their wisdom, strength or achievements? It could be a singer who energizes you with their music or lyrics, a sportsperson, a campaigner for justice, someone who has coped through illness or difficult life events, or a religious or historical figure. How might this person advise or encourage you?

You can also turn to the natural world. Can you think of an animal who seems wise and understanding or who makes you feel brave, strong and powerful? Can you imagine sitting by them and looking into their eyes for support and advice? Would being in nature inspire your Wise Mind? Can you think about an amazing view, sitting in a park or garden, staring out to sea or gazing down from a high mountain across a lake? How would this affect how you see the world?

Make a note of whatever images or ideas seem helpful to encourage your own Wise Mind to speak up a little more and find ways to help and support you through tough times.

....

....

....

 Pause and Think   10 Minutes

Ask your Wise Mind for advice

Now you have some ideas and images, you can start to ask your Wise Mind for advice and guidance to help you make wise choices about what to do and how to cope when you start to feel anxious.

Think of a situation that makes you feel a little anxious or lacking in confidence. What thoughts show up when you think about this?

....

....

....

174

Now, bring up your image for Wise Mind and use this to help you answer these questions.

What would Wise Mind say? Think about the most supportive teacher, coach or friend and how they might encourage or motivate you.	
What would you say to a friend or family member who was struggling with the same situation? What could you say that's friendly, helpful or encouraging?	
Where is your Guide pointing? What's most important to you about this situation?	
You can choose helpful actions, even if you feel anxious or fearful. What wise choices can you make that might help you cope with this situation? What's the first micro-step you can take?	

Archie says: For my Wise Mind, I chose a polar bear. They are really strong and powerful and good at looking after themselves in harsh conditions. This morning I was starting to worry about going to school and all the things that might go wrong during the day. I started thinking I should take the day off. Then, I imagined the polar bear walking with me to school and staying next to me all day, giving me the confidence to speak up more in lessons. I took a breath and did 54321. This helped my anxiety to settle down and I decided I would go in because there are some important lessons today.

 Do This  10 Minutes

Dealing with anxious thoughts

When your Anxiety Alarm is switched on or you have become stuck on the Worry Roundabout, it's easy to get caught up in anxious thoughts and see the world as a dangerous and scary place. You can use Wise Mind to help find a more balanced and helpful point of view. Here are some different ways to do this. Can you choose two or three ideas and try them out?

Use a revolving door

You don't have to talk back, argue, convince or even listen to your anxious thoughts. Instead, allow them to come in and out through a revolving door.

When they appear, you can greet them in a friendly way: 'Hi Scaremonger! Hello Worry-Worm! I see you have both shown up today.' Then, take a slow breath, create some space inside and allow them to wander back out of your mind when they are ready!

Don't let the thoughts distract you from following your Guide. Can you move on and do something else more important?

Thoughts on a TV screen

Imagine that you can see your thoughts flashing up on a TV screen. Instead of watching in full colour on a giant screen, can you imagine that the screen shrinks down to the size of your phone? The movie and soundtrack are still playing, but it's much smaller and quieter and you can start to notice other things around you. Maybe it could start playing at double speed, or even turn into a cartoon with silly voices! This can make the thoughts seem less believable. Even if the movie is still playing, you can put the phone in your pocket and carry on with your day.

Take a helicopter view

Think of a situation that makes you feel just a little anxious. Pick something that doesn't trigger strong emotions or panic. Ask yourself: What makes me anxious about this? What do I worry will happen?

Now imagine jumping into a helicopter and rising high up into the air where you can see things more clearly and with less intensity. Ask yourself these questions.

Widen your perspective	What happens as you start to rise and see things from high above or a broader viewpoint? Can you see anything new? How might it seem to someone who isn't involved in the situation?	
Take the test of time	How might you see the situation in two weeks, six months or a year from now? What about in five or ten years?	

Is this helpful?	Is the way you are thinking about the situation helping you to be the person you want to be and to do the things you care about?	
Let go of certainty	Can you be more willing to accept not knowing what is ahead? It could be exciting, adventurous, spontaneous and thrilling!	
Focus on what's important	Where is your Guide pointing? What wise actions can you choose that link to what matters most?	

Find an ARC to bridge difficult experiences

You can also imagine Wise Mind as an **ARC** or a bridge helping you over a wild, swirling river. The river includes all the scary thoughts, feelings, body sensations and urges to escape that show up when you start feeling anxious. The bridge is the point that you have *choice*. Using the bridge allows you to make wise choices, take wise actions and cross over towards what you care about. This can free you from feeling trapped by anxiety and fear and take you across the river towards where you want to go:

→ **Allow the thoughts and feelings:** Take a moment to pause and to notice and name what thoughts and feelings have shown up: 'I'm feeling anxious, scared, panicky... I'm thinking about how embarrassing it will be if I make a mistake in front of everyone...'

→ **Recognize your urge to react:** Let out one or two long slow breaths and notice any impulses to react to these uncomfortable thoughts and feelings: 'I feel like running away and hiding in my bedroom and never coming out again!'

→ **Choose a wise action:** Take another slow breath and allow the negative thoughts and feelings to pass. Now ask your Wise Mind for advice. Can you choose a wise action? What choices would help you to follow your Guide and become the person you want to be, even when you are experiencing anxiety, discomfort and distress?

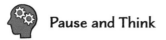 **Pause and Think**  **10 Minutes**

Work through a Worry Plan

Another useful skill for dealing with anxiety is to use a Worry Plan. This will help you decide whether a worry is something that you have some control over and you can take some action on, or whether it's just something that *might* happen or that you cannot control.

If you can do something about the worry, you can use problem-solving to think about what action to take, and then make a plan to do this. Turn back to Chapter 5 for a reminder about the problem-solving steps.

If you can't do anything about the problem right away, or the worry is about something that you can't control, then it's not helpful to spend too much time thinking about it over and over again. Instead, you can use techniques such as 54321 to shift your focus away from worries and just allow them to pass back out of your mind when they are ready. Try to bring your attention to something else that is important. We talk more about ways to cope with worry in Chapter 7.

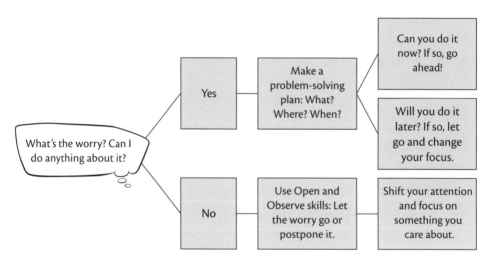

Plan ways to cope

Anxiety and worry often involve repeated 'what if...?' thoughts about possible future problems, such as:

What if... I look foolish in front of my friends?

What if... I make a mistake, or something goes wrong?

What if... I get sick?

What if... I make the wrong decision?

Managing worry shouldn't just be about trying to reassure yourself that the worst won't happen. Instead, it's often more helpful to focus on building your self-belief and confidence that you can cope if something scary or difficult happens.

Think of one worry or a 'what if...?' thought and make a note of it here:

My worry is what if...?

....

....

....

....

....

Now, ask yourself: 'Then what could I do? If things did go wrong, how could I cope?' Use the following questions to help guide your answer.

What skills or experience do you have that might help you cope even if something goes wrong?	
What help, advice or support could you get from other people?	
What practical steps could you take that would make a start in dealing with any problems that happen?	
How much time are you spending on this worry? Is it stopping you from doing anything else important?	
What does your Wise Mind say? Where is your Guide pointing? What's the most helpful thing you can do next?	

Archie says: I do have a lot of 'what if...?' worry thoughts! I usually try to reassure myself or ask my parents, but I can see that this often doesn't last long and I just end up worrying again.

Today my worry was: What if I mess up my maths test at school tomorrow?

What skills or experience do you have that might help you cope even if something goes wrong?	*I have good grades and I have a good report from my maths teacher.*
What help, advice or support could you get from other people?	*I could take a look at the questions tonight and ask my parents or a friend if I'm not sure what to do.*
What practical steps could you take that would make a start in dealing with any problems that happen?	*If I don't do brilliantly in the test, it's not the end of the world and I could ask my teacher for help to find out what went wrong.*
How much time are you spending on this worry? Is it stopping you from doing anything else important?	*I'm spending a lot of time thinking about this and it's stopping me relaxing and enjoying the evening.*
What does your Wise Mind say? Where is your Guide pointing? What's the most helpful thing you can do next?	*My Wise Mind reminded me that usually I do fine on tests, and constant worrying will not help me to do any better. I'm going to spend an hour revising but then I will go out to my Scout group instead of staying home and thinking about the test all evening.*

Remember your skills, strengths and qualities

Another way to use your Wise Mind is to remember all your skills and abilities, accomplishments and the qualities that make you unique. Has someone ever told you that you're smart? Funny? Kind? Artistic? A caring friend? A good student? A talented writer? A promising athlete?

Do you acknowledge these compliments, or do you brush them off? Thinking about your strengths might feel a little uncomfortable at first. You may not be used to focusing on your qualities and finding the good in yourself, and you might spend more time beating yourself up for your flaws.

This exercise is not about being vain, it's about seeing the real you – and making sure you don't ignore the parts you can be proud of. If you find it difficult, you can ask a supportive friend or relative for help.

Complete the table with some of your strengths and qualities.

What are some of your strengths?	
What are you good at?	
What do you enjoy and care about?	
How can you appreciate and use these qualities in your life even more?	

 Pause and Think **10 Minutes**

Your strengths checklist

Your strengths are not just related to your achievements but include many other important qualities such as being honest, trustworthy, fair and caring for others. Look at the list below and choose at least four or five strengths and qualities that you can recognize. Choose a recent example of each one and then think about how you can appreciate or develop this quality:

Strengths and qualities checklist	What is a recent example of this?	How can you expand or grow this quality or use it in your life?
I was caring and friendly.		
I was fair and honest.		
I acted as a leader.		
I was interested in something.		
I understood someone else's point of view.		

cont.

Strengths and qualities checklist	What is a recent example of this?	How can you expand or grow this quality or use it in your life?
I learned something new.		
I worked hard or overcame an obstacle or problem.		
I gave good advice or support to someone.		
I coped with some difficult emotions or thoughts.		
I was energetic and active.		
I was careful or planned ahead.		
I was brave in the face of stress or danger.		
I spoke up for what was right.		
I was creative.		
I forgave someone else, or myself.		
I understood a fact or some information.		
I had fun or brought a smile to someone's face.		
I completed something.		

Archie says: It felt weird to think about my good qualities, but it was nice to think about something more positive for a change. I found it quite hard, so I asked my best friend for help. He said that I'm a thoughtful and supportive friend. It felt good to think about some of the important qualities that I care about a lot. It reminded me that life's not just about doing well in sports or at school!

Summary: Wise Mind

➜ Listening to your Wise Mind involves looking at the big picture and being friendly, fair and supportive as you encourage yourself to face challenges and uncertainty.

➜ Noticing and naming your anxious thoughts can make them less powerful.

➜ You use a revolving door for negative thoughts, shrink them on a screen or take a helicopter view of difficult situations.

➜ When anxious thoughts or feelings show up, you can choose wise actions that follow your Guide and move you towards things that matter.

➜ Working through a Worry Plan and planning ways to cope with problems can build your confidence and reduce your anxiety.

Final thoughts

Make a note of anything you have found helpful, interesting or surprising from this chapter.

....

....

....

....

....

....

....

What are you going to do now? Can you choose one small action for the coming week based on what you have discovered from this chapter?

....

....

....

....

....

....

Chapter 15

TREAT YOURSELF KINDLY

Zachary: I set myself very high standards and it's often hard to live up to these. Even making a small mistake feels like a huge failure and I'm always living in fear that I won't do as well as I'd hoped. It feels exhausting and stressful. Then, things got worse last year when I was bullied at school by a group of lads. They would shout things at me, call me names and sometimes push or trip me up. I started getting anxious that I might run into them. If I had to go to the canteen, I would get a pounding heart, butterflies in my tummy and my breathing was fast. I started getting panic attacks in the morning before going to school. I lost a lot of confidence and started to believe that there must be something wrong with me. I stopped going to after-school clubs and spent a lot of time by myself feeling lonely, isolated and anxious.

When you spend a lot of time feeling anxious or worried, you may also start to see yourself negatively or give yourself a hard time. You might compare yourself negatively to others or blame yourself for your problems. You find yourself saying things like 'Why am I so anxious all the time? I'm such a mess! Why can't I do better? I'm a complete loser!'

Things can be especially difficult when you are coping with problems such as bullying, discrimination or abuse. The impact of other people's cruel or unkind behaviour can become an even bigger issue if you begin echoing the negative voices and telling yourself the same critical messages. But saying unkind things to yourself can be just as hurtful and damaging as saying them to someone else. Repeatedly getting into a habit of blaming and criticizing yourself can have a huge impact on your self-confidence, making your anxiety a bigger problem.

You might also feel anxious because you have unrealistic expectations of yourself or set unreachable targets. Do you constantly strive for perfection and tell yourself that you've failed if even something small goes wrong? Do you need to be liked by everyone and tell yourself that you are worthless if you have fallen out with a friend?

In this chapter, we will:

→ discover your three emotion systems and how these can influence your mind and body

→ learn how treating yourself with kindness can help you cope with anxiety and become better able to cope under pressure

→ practise ways to Treat yourself Kindly and become a better friend to yourself.

 Read This   5 Minutes

The three emotion systems

→ Three different emotion systems can affect your body and mind and will influence your feelings and reactions in different situations. Each system is important, and they work together to help you feel happy and content, and to enable you to cope with stressful life events and challenges. The three emotion systems are:

 Read This   10 Minutes

Threat system

We have already learned about the Threat system in the first few chapters of this book. As a quick reminder, the Threat system is your survival system, and its job is to alert you to any possible danger and to keep you safe from harm. Whenever you face any kind of stressful or threatening situation, your Threat system will wake up and take action. By releasing hormones such as adrenaline and cortisol, it tells your body to take immediate action and stay safe.

When the Threat system is activated, you will often experience Fight Flight Freeze reactions:

→ **Fight:** you get ready to defend yourself and combat the danger.

→ **Flight:** you try to avoid, escape or run away from the danger. You might also try to stay safe by constantly checking for danger or staying close to someone else.

→ **Freeze:** You feel stuck, frozen and unable to move as you stay completely still to avoid detection and prevent attention from being drawn to you.

You can experience many different emotions when the Threat system is activated, including fear, anger, disgust, embarrassment and shame. Your body will start preparing to take Fight Flight Freeze actions, so you may notice that your heart is thumping in your chest, you breathe faster, you start sweating, shaking, feeling sick or get a tummy ache.

Is your Threat system too touchy?

The Threat system is designed to respond quickly to unexpected danger. It can be activated by many threats in the outside world, such as when you are facing a bully or taking a difficult exam. The Threat system will also step in to save you if you need to jump out of the path of a speeding car to avoid being run over.

When you become anxious, you may find that your Threat system is switched on more easily. Your brain starts to exaggerate risks and you may worry about problems that are unlikely to happen. The Threat system can also be triggered by harsh and self-critical thoughts that go through your mind, such as when you give yourself a hard time for being anxious, and tell yourself how useless or stupid you are.

Living with a touchy Threat system can make you feel on edge, jumpy and exhausted. It can affect your memory and learning and make it harder to relax and enjoy yourself, even if there are no dangers to deal with.

Pause and Think **5 Minutes**

Observe your Threat system

Answer the following questions about your Threat system:

How sensitive or 'touchy' is your Threat system? What happens in your body when it is set off? What feelings does it bring?	
What problems, stresses or difficulties in the outside world often set off your Threat system?	
Do you ever trigger your Threat system by giving yourself a hard time or calling yourself harsh or unkind names? How do you feel when this happens? How does this affect your actions?	

 Do This **5 Minutes**

Turn down your Threat system

You can view your Threat system as an over-sensitive alarm, rather than something bad. You can **Notice the NOW** whenever you need to create a pause and turn down the volume of your threat system. We first met this technique in Chapter 1:

→ **N**otice that your Threat system has switched on and how this is affecting your body and mind. *I am feeling tense and stressed. My chest is tight, and my heart is thumping. I'm having lots of thoughts about how I messed up my lines at the play rehearsal tonight.*

→ **O**bserve your body and the world around, using your five senses. Name two or three things that you can see, hear, feel, taste and smell. Describe

all these things in your mind: *I am sitting in a room with a blue chair and grey curtains. I can feel my feet on the floor and the soft seat on my chair. I can hear the buzz of my computer. I can smell and taste the toast I am eating. I can notice the here and now.* Take three slow breaths in and out from deep within your belly, noticing all the sensations involved in taking those breaths. *I feel my belly swelling, I feel the cool air coming through my nose and I feel my muscles softening.*

→ **W**hat's important? In this pause, check in with Wise Mind and your Guide. What's most important to do next? Move on to do this with as much attention as you can. *I'm going to watch this TV programme and focus on the storyline. I'm going to chat with my friend and pay attention to what she's saying.*

Zachary says: I'm getting even more tired and stressed as my exams are getting closer. My Threat system is switched on the whole time when it comes to schoolwork! I'm worried about messing up one of the papers and getting a bad grade. I'm working harder and harder, but that just makes me more tired and it's hard to concentrate. I tried using Notice the NOW to take a break from all the stress and anxiety. It wasn't easy, but afterwards, I felt a little bit calmer, and my mind was more settled. I decided that I'd done enough studying for the day and to take a break and go for an evening walk with my mum. I'll get back to revising tomorrow!

 Read This 10 Minutes

Drive system

Your Drive system is how your body and brain motivate you to get things done. Activating Drive involves seeking out the things that you want and need to survive and enjoy life. These include friendship, food, treats or success at school or in sports. Every time you pass a test, win a competition or achieve any goal that you have set for yourself, you engage the Drive system and will experience positive feelings of pleasure, excitement and satisfaction.

The Drive system encourages you to focus on actions that lead to important goals and helps you to build positive relationships with others. When it's in balance with the other systems, Drive helps to build your confidence and self-belief, and leads to success in many different areas of life.

Activating your Drive system can create a 'buzz' of excitement which feels enjoyable as you achieve any goal you have set for yourself. However, if you use your Drive system too much, you can get stuck in 'over-drive' where you are trying to do too much and are too focused on achievement without allowing yourself time to rest or have fun. This can lead to a racing mind, problems with sleep and difficulty relaxing or winding down so you get worn out and tired.

Drive can also be linked to uncomfortable feelings. Sometimes, your Threat and Drive systems may join forces and you start to see people or situations as threatening or critical. If your desires and goals are blocked, this can also feel like a threat and lead to feelings of frustration, anger and stress.

If you cut down or avoid enjoyable or important activities due to feeling anxious or low, then you may not use your Drive system enough – you become stuck in 'under-drive'. By doing less of the things that matter to you, you lose the pleasure and satisfaction that come from activating your Drive system regularly. You feel more fed up and anxious and can lose confidence in your ability to achieve even small goals.

 Pause and Think **5 Minutes**

Notice your Drive system

Can you think of a time when you activated your Drive system and achieved something, even very small? How did it feel to do this?	
Do you ever get stuck in 'over-drive' where you push yourself too hard to get things done? Do you get over-focused on one task? How does this affect how you live your life?	

Do you ever get stuck in 'under-drive' where you are not regularly activating your Drive system and find it hard to get past your anxiety or motivate yourself to get things done? How does this affect your mood, sense of achievement and purpose in life?

 Do This  5 Minutes

Balance your Drive system

Here are some tips for balancing your Drive system:

Tip for balancing your Drive system	How could you use this? What can you do?
Observe your Drive system: Notice how much time you spend each day focusing on goals or achievements. Can you find a balance between 'over-drive' and 'under-drive'? Try to aim for just the right amount of activity for you.	
Check in with your Guide and Wise Mind: Remind yourself of all the things that are important to you and make sure that your activities are balanced and move you towards what you care about. Keep all your different values in mind, such as enjoyment, relaxation or connection with friends and family.	
Plan a micro-step: If you are struggling to overcome anxiety, or to motivate yourself and activate your Drive system, try planning a really small and achievable goal. Turn back to Chapter 12 if you need a reminder of how to do this.	

Zachary says: Since I was bullied, it's been harder to motivate myself to do much at all, except for studying. I'm sinking into 'under-drive' – thinking about all the activities I used to do regularly feels overwhelming and difficult. I spend a lot of time by myself, often just lying down in my bedroom, worrying about everything and thinking how useless I am for being unable to cope with life.

Today I made a real effort to remind myself about my Guide and to plan a few micro-steps that might wake up my Drive system and create more sense of achievement. I have some weights in the cupboard, and I haven't touched them for months. I decided to spend 10 minutes doing a strength workout. I had to lift much lighter weights than I used to, but it felt good to achieve something. Being stronger helps me to believe in myself a bit more. I'd love to build back up to going to the gym or to rugby training again once I have a bit more confidence.

Being fair to yourself

Using your Drive system wisely involves setting yourself interesting and exciting goals that follow your Guide and expand your life. Having high standards for yourself, such as 'I like to do things well' and 'It's important to try my hardest' can give you a sense of accomplishment and boost your self-esteem. But it can also create pressure if your expectations and demands on yourself are too harsh.

It's important that your goals are fair and realistic, and that you can relax or adapt them when facing a complicated or challenging situation. If your standards are too high, or you constantly want things to be absolutely 'right', it may be impossible to live up to them, so you are setting yourself up to fail. You might also start to feel that you are not capable of doing enough or being 'good enough' and lose confidence in your abilities.

High levels of stress, anxiety and fear of failure can also make it harder to get things done. You may start to feel overwhelmed, put off getting started, work more slowly or have trouble making even small decisions.

 Pause and Think **5 Minutes**

Can you treat yourself more fairly?

Here are some of our tips for ways to treat yourself fairly and use your Drive system wisely. Look at these tips and write down some ways you can think of to use them.

Make your goal smaller: If you are feeling overwhelmed or overburdened by difficult tasks and demands, can you make your goal smaller or easier to achieve? Or can you seek some support to achieve it?

Focus on the process not the outcome: Set yourself a goal to get more involved or to try out an activity rather than to be 'good at it'. For example, plan to be just a little more active during the week without setting goals about how far or fast you 'should' run or swim.

Do things just for fun: Try doing something because you have always wanted to try it rather than because you are good at it or are striving for achievement or praise.

Relax your expectations: Can you relax a standard or expectation just a little? Can you aim for silver or bronze rather than a gold medal and try doing something to an 'OK' or 'good enough' standard? What would this look like?

Zachary says: I can see that the amount of stress and pressure that I put myself under is probably making it harder for me to do things. In sports, I feel so anxious to do well that I sometimes freeze and can't remember any of my training. I've even been avoiding going to practice because I feel so worried about my performance. I love sports and I want to carry on, but I am going to try to relax my expectations and focus on the activity rather than how well I do. If I focus on enjoying myself, I think it will be better, and even if things don't go well, at least I will have more fun doing the activity!

Calm and Connect system

The Calm and Connect system is how you switch off and recover from anxiety and stress. This system helps to turn down the volume of the Threat system, allowing you to recharge and settle down after experiencing uncomfortable or distressing feelings of anxiety. When the Calm and Connect system is switched on, you feel relaxed, your heart rate slows and you feel peaceful and safe. It also helps you to connect with those who care about you, bringing feelings of affection and helping to soothe strong emotions in yourself and those around you.

When you are living with anxiety and your Threat system is on constant red alert, you may find that the Calm and Connect system gets turned down too low, or that you hardly use it at all. This means that the Threat system continues sounding the alarm and you feel anxious, tense and agitated, even if you are not sure why. Without the balancing effect of the Calm and Connect system, you may also react by becoming critical and blaming yourself for feeling anxious, which can lead to feelings of shame and sadness, along with many painful and self-critical thoughts.

Sometimes, your Calm and Connect system may become linked to your Threat system. This can happen if those who are supposed to care for you are also frightening or abusive, so the behaviours and emotions that are usually linked to feelings of caring or safety can trigger a sense of fear and threat rather than safety. An example of this could be if you misinterpret a friend's gesture of support when they offer to help you with an assignment and you feel angry or ashamed, thinking that they see you as stupid or incapable.

 Do This ⏰ 10 Minutes

Supercharge your Calm and Connect system

There are many ways to switch on your Calm and Connect system. It might come from the sense of connection you feel as you chat with a friend after a tough day. Or you might decide to relax in a warm bath and enjoy listening to calming music as a way of winding down.

It's important to make time to actively use your Calm and Connect system, as it's easy for it to be ignored or forgotten when you have a busy or active life. When you remember to plug it in and put it 'on charge', you are likely to feel more balanced and content, and less anxious or agitated. Here are some of our tips on ways to supercharge your Calm and Connect system.

Tips for supercharging your Calm and Connect system	How can you use this? What can you do?
Connect with a supportive tribe: Who makes you feel warm, safe and accepted? Make sure that you regularly spend time with people who are encouraging and want the best for you.	
Try a calming activity: Even 5–10 minutes of a relaxing activity such as taking a bath, reading, knitting, doing a jigsaw, yoga, painting or stroking your pet or a soft blanket, can all strengthen your Calm and Connect system and bring a little peacefulness into your day.	
Go into nature: Take a few minutes to notice and appreciate the outside world – look at the sky, a tall tree or an amazing view. Use your senses to appreciate the moment – what can you see, hear, feel and smell?	

cont.

Tips for supercharging your Calm and Connect system	How can you use this? What can you do?
Practise your Open and Observe skills: Being more present and mindful will strengthen your Calm and Connect system. Why not take a few slow breaths or practise relaxation? You can turn back to Chapter 13 for a reminder of some ideas to try.	
Find three things you can appreciate in the world, however small: *The sun is shining, I enjoyed my sandwich at lunchtime, and my friend gave me a birthday card.*	

 Read This  10 Minutes

Being a friend to yourself

Learning to switch on your Calm and Connect system often involves becoming just a little kinder and more encouraging as you become a good friend to yourself, just as you are to other people. This involves using your Wise Mind, which we learned about in Chapter 14.

There are several important ways to become a really good friend to yourself. You can:

→ **Have a friendly and encouraging attitude:** This involves being kind, understanding and accepting yourself for who you are. It's also about having fair and realistic expectations of yourself and remembering that you are not superhuman or indestructible but just doing your best in an imperfect and complicated world.

→ **Observe what's happening inside:** This involves stepping back and noticing any uncomfortable thoughts and feelings that show up without being stuck in them or believing that these are the only ways to view the world. You can turn back to Chapter 13 for some ideas on how to do this.

→ **Look at the big picture:** Connect with your Wise Mind and remember that you are not alone and that many others are coping with similar experiences, feelings and challenges. This is also about being fair to yourself and keeping in mind all of your strengths, abilities and things that have gone well in life, as well as anything that has been difficult or gone wrong.

→ **Practise problem-solving:** This involves seeing difficulties as a normal part of life and looking for ways to overcome them rather than criticizing and blaming yourself or 'kicking yourself when you are down'. Turn to Chapter 5 for more ideas about how to do this.

→ **Choose kind actions:** Plan micro-actions to care for yourself, such as making yourself a relaxing drink, or choosing a healthy snack because you care about your body. Don't let these get squeezed out of your day because you are anxious, busy or feeling fed up.

→ **Stand tall:** Know that you matter and learn to notice and speak up when situations or people lack respect, equality or care for you and others.

 Pause and Think 10 Minutes

Become your own best friend

Look at the table below for some ways that you could switch on your Calm and Connect system and treat yourself with kindness. Which of these can you start to use in your own life?

Become your own friend	Examples of what to try	Can you use this? What could you do?
Friendly and encouraging attitude	Put a sticky note in your bedroom with a reminder to be kind when you need it. Use the same words to talk to yourself as you would to a friend. When something goes wrong, instead of name-calling or self-criticism, take a short pause and then ask your Wise Mind for friendly advice.	

cont.

Become your own friend	Examples of what to try	Can you use this? What could you do?
Observe what's happening inside	When feeling scared, angry or ashamed, try taking a few slow breaths. Notice and name any difficult thoughts and feelings. Place a hand over your heart or wrap your arms around your shoulders and give yourself a hug. Imagine your hands are filled with warmth and kindness. Tell yourself: *This is tough. I care about you and I'm on your side. I'll help you get through this.*	
Look at the big picture	Pause and zoom out of the scary details of a problem or difficult situation. Remind yourself of your strengths and abilities and all your past achievements.	
Practise problem-solving	Make a list of problems you are facing and brainstorm ideas for how you could deal with these. What's the first tiny step you could take?	
Choose kind actions	Find 10 minutes to read a book, do some drawing, sit in the park, practise yoga, take a restful bath or spend time with people that you care about.	
Stand tall	Express your feelings and the things that are important to you calmly and fairly. Call out discrimination or injustice when you see it. Be willing to set boundaries and say 'no' when you need to.	

Zachary says: It feels weird to think about being a better friend to myself because I'm used to giving myself a hard time or being on the receiving end of insults from bullies. But I'm making an effort to remind myself that I'm not so bad, I'm doing the best I can and I can keep trying even when things are hard. I wrote it on a Post-it note and pinned it to my mirror so I see it every morning. I also decided to try to turn up the volume of my Calm and Connect system. I have found that listening to a short mindfulness track on an app can help to settle me when I'm feeling anxious or worried, so I'm going to try doing this for a few minutes every day.

Chapter summary

→ Saying negative or self-critical things to yourself is just as hurtful as saying them to another person.

→ Three emotion systems affect your body and mind and will influence how you react to different situations:

> **Threat:** This survival system helps you react quickly to cope with possible danger using Fight Flight Freeze reactions.

> **Drive:** Motivates you to seek out accomplishments and get things done.

> **Calm and Connect:** Allows you to feel calm, peaceful and safe and to recover from stress.

→ Being a friend to yourself involves being kind, encouraging and friendly, setting fair expectations, practising problem-solving and standing up for yourself when needed.

Final thoughts
Make a note of anything you have found helpful, interesting or surprising from this chapter.

....
....
....

....

....

....

What are you going to do now? Can you choose one small action for the coming week based on what you have discovered from this chapter?

....

....

....

....

....

....

Chapter 16

HEALTHY LIFE HABITS

When you are feeling anxious, worried or panicky, it's common to make changes in your daily habits, such as sleep, exercise, activity and eating patterns. This can often have a negative effect on your wellbeing and may worsen how you feel. Lack of sleep and a poor diet leave you feeling exhausted and tense, and affect your immune system and general health, making it harder to concentrate, think clearly or make decisions. It becomes harder to follow your Guide and do the important things, but by avoiding these you can feel increasingly anxious, demotivated and fed up.

In this chapter, we will explore how creating a routine with Healthy Life Habits can improve your anxiety and increase your happiness and wellbeing.

These habits include:

→ healthy eating patterns

→ being physically active

→ getting enough sleep

→ cutting back on unhealthy choices such as smoking or vaping, drinking alcohol and taking drugs, or overuse of technology.

 Pause and Think   **10 Minutes**

What are your life habits right now?

Take a moment to think about your current life habits. What's helpful or healthy for you? Is there anything that you would like to change or improve?

Life habits or patterns	What are you doing already that's healthy or helpful?	What would you like to change or improve?
Healthy eating: Do you have regular eating patterns and a balance of healthy nutrition that works for your body and lifestyle? Are you able to keep a healthy weight?		
Physical activity: Are you active during the day or do you spend a lot of time sitting or lying down? How much exercise do you do each week?		
Sleep: Do you have regular sleep habits and usually wake up feeling rested? How easy is it to drop off? Do you stay asleep through the night?		
Other life habits: Do you have any unhealthy habits such as smoking, vaping, drinking too much alcohol or taking drugs? Do you have healthy technology or screen habits?		

 **Read This** 10 Minutes

Healthy eating habits

> **Freya:** I probably don't eat as healthily as I should. When I'm feeling anxious or worried about something, I often feel quite sick or bloated, so I find myself skipping meals. Then I get hungry later and find myself turning to sugary junk food or crisps for a quick boost. Lately, I've been feeling really tired and lacking energy and I think my eating patterns are a big part of this.

Healthy eating is important for taking care of your body and mind. A healthy diet is essential for growth and development, helps you keep a healthy weight and provides energy to enjoy your daily activities. Making healthy eating choices can boost your confidence and self-esteem as you feel a sense of pride from knowing you are making active choices to take care of yourself. In the long term, healthy eating habits can reduce your risks of health conditions such as diabetes and heart disease.

When you are feeling anxious, you may notice changes in your appetite or enjoyment of food. Some people turn to food as a comfort for emotional distress, which can lead to cravings for sugary or high-fat junk foods. These may be enjoyable in the short term but have unhealthy consequences if they become a regular or frequent habit. If you are not eating enough, then you may start to feel tired or develop headaches or dizziness which make it harder to do the activities that are important for wellbeing.

 **Read This** 5 Minutes

If this is a topic that you find triggering or distressing, you can simply skip this section and move on to the other Healthy Life Habits.

Eating disorders

It's important to recognize if you are struggling with an eating disorder, which can affect your physical health and emotional wellbeing. Common eating disorders include anorexia nervosa, bulimia nervosa and binge eating.

If eating makes you feel anxious, guilty or upset, or you are restricting your food intake or changing your eating patterns because of difficult emotions or concerns about your appearance, it is important to recognize this and take action as there are effective treatments available. We recommend talking to your doctor or seeking support from an adult that you trust.

 Pause and Think **10 Minutes**

Healthy eating checklist

A healthy diet will usually contain a range of foods from each of the different food groups. You don't need to achieve this with every meal, but it's helpful to try and find a balance over a day or week.

Look at the following checklist of ways to follow a healthy diet that can improve your anxiety and wellbeing.

Healthy eating checklist	What can you continue doing? What do you need to change?
Eat for energy, with regular meals throughout the day to provide fuel for your body and brain. Don't skip meals, and have healthy snacks to boost energy levels if you are using more brain or body power.	
Starchy carbohydrates such as potatoes, bread, rice and pasta are a good source of energy. Try to include high-fibre varieties such as whole-wheat pasta, brown rice and wholemeal bread.	
Choose more fruits and vegetables, which contain a range of vitamins and minerals that your body needs to function well.	

Include some protein with each meal such as fish, meat, poultry, eggs, pulses and seeds or nuts.	
Drink water with every meal and throughout the day rather than sugary soft drinks or fruit juice. This will hydrate you and can help to balance your appetite and food intake.	
Cut down on processed or packaged foods and keep a limit on foods high in sugar, fat or salt, such as fizzy drinks, crisps, cakes and chocolate. You don't have to give these up completely but try to eat them less often and in small amounts.	

Healthy eating tips

Here are a few more ideas to improve your healthy eating habits.

Healthy eating habit	How could you use this tip? What will you do differently?
Connect with others at mealtimes: Create a habit of regularly eating with your family. Turn meals into a social event that is a time to talk as well as to eat. This can be a great way to share anything that's worrying you. How about banning mobile phones from the dinner table to encourage the conversation?	

cont.

Healthy eating habit	How could you use this tip? What will you do differently?
Plan ahead and banish junk food: Filling your cupboards with healthy foods such as fruit, nuts, yoghurt and wholemeal bread will make it easier to make healthy choices when you are tired or hungry. Try making your packed lunch the night before, including a healthy snack for break time. Keep unhealthy snacks as an occasional treat rather than a regular habit.	
Get more involved: Begin to plan, shop for and cook meals for yourself and the family. This can be fun and will give you more control over your food choices. Why not experiment with a new dish or ingredient?	

Freya: I started making an effort to have breakfast every day, and I found that eating a slice of wholemeal toast helps settle my tummy when I'm feeling anxious. I also try to have more regular meals with my family and to make sure I put my phone down and talk to my parents and my sisters. It has made me feel closer and more connected to them, and it also gives me a chance to talk through anything that's on my mind. I'm definitely going to keep it up!

 Read This  10 Minutes

Healthy sleep habits

Kanye: Sleep has become a big problem for me, especially since I've been feeling more anxious. I often lie awake worrying about things that happened during the day or things that might go wrong in the future. In the morning, I feel exhausted and fed up. It's hard to get up and even harder to concentrate during the day because I'm so tired and my mind just goes back to all the worries that kept me awake.

We all need good sleep. It's essential for rest and recuperation, growth and development, and emotional and physical wellbeing. Everyone is different but, on the whole, 8–10 hours of sleep per night is about right for most young people aged 11–24. Not getting enough sleep can have many effects on your body and mind, and can lead to anxiety, low mood, problems with performance and concentration, reduced creativity, weight gain and lowered immunity to illness.

Many things can interfere with a good night's sleep. Sleep problems may be triggered by life stresses and worries about exams, homework, relationships, social activities or jobs. Anxiety can also affect your sleep, making it harder to drop off, or you may find yourself waking in the early hours thinking about problems so that you feel tired and unrefreshed in the morning. You might find that your sleep is less refreshing and you feel constantly exhausted and lacking in energy or enthusiasm.

Your sleep patterns are controlled by your body's internal biological clock known as a 'circadian rhythm'. Your body clock is affected by light and temperature and is also influenced by activity and eating patterns. When it's bright outside, you feel more alert and awake, and when it becomes dark, the body releases hormones such as melatonin, which makes you feel sleepy.

As you enter the teenage years, your circadian rhythm can change quite dramatically. You may find that your body clock tells you to go to bed later and to wake up much later than before. Unfortunately, this shift does not always match the school timetable or your social calendar. It's important to keep your activity and sleep patterns balanced through the week and not try and 'catch up' on missed sleep at weekends.

Your sleep can also be affected by stimulants such as caffeine, nicotine, alcohol and drugs. Alcohol and certain drugs often become a 'false friend' – making you relaxed and sleepy at bedtime, but you then wake early or have disturbed sleep that is less refreshing.

 Pause and Think   **10 Minutes**

How is your sleep?
The occasional poor night of sleep is completely normal. However, if you've been sleeping badly for a few weeks or longer, this may be a good time to look at what is causing the disturbance and make a change. The first step is to keep track of your sleep amount and quality over one or two weeks.

Day/Date							
What time did you go to sleep?							
What time did you wake up?							
Rate the quality of your sleep from 1 to 10. How rested or energetic did you feel afterwards?							
Notes: What things might have affected your sleep (helpful or unhelpful)? Was there any change to your routine?							

Pause and Think **10 Minutes**

Technology and sleep

Are your technology habits interfering with your sleep? Checking messages, using social media or playing computer games late at night can make you feel agitated and wakeful, triggering worries and anxiety, and making it harder to drop off to sleep. Smartphones, tablets, computers and television screens also give off short-wavelength blue light, which can trick the body into thinking it's still daytime and make you more alert at night.

Look at some of our technology tips for improving sleep.

Sleep tips and screen use	Could you try this? What could you do?
Cut down on late-night use of electronic devices, especially those which are held close to your face, such as phones and tablets.	
Curb the temptation to check your phone, social media account or news items that are likely to trigger your anxiety around bedtime or at night.	
Charge your phone in another room or turn it off overnight so that incoming messages and notifications don't affect your sleep and you are less tempted to use it at night.	
Dim the screen or use a night mode with warmer tones in the evening.	
Listen to a relaxing audiobook rather than watching a screen at bedtime.	

 **Read This** **10 Minutes**

Tips for improving sleep

There are many things you can do to improve your sleep. Take a look at these tips for getting better sleep and managing anxiety and worry at night. Can you choose two or three things to try out?

I have trouble getting to sleep.	**Set a regular sleep pattern:** Stick to similar times for going to bed and waking up each day and avoid sleeping in too long after a bad night's sleep or on weekends.
	Create a 'wind-down' routine: Plan a relaxing activity to prepare your body and mind for sleep, such as reading, listening to music, having a bath or doing yoga.
	Make a 'sleep haven': Ensure your bedroom is dark, quiet, not too cluttered, that your bed is comfortable and the room is a good temperature for sleeping.
	Cut out daytime naps: The odd nap after a late night is fine, but don't let this become a regular habit. If you need to nap, make it short (15 minutes or less) and before 3 pm.
	Reduce caffeine, nicotine, alcohol or other stimulants, especially within 6 hours of bedtime. Avoid heavy meals late at night.
	Cover the clock: Checking the time can lead to worry and impatience. Set the alarm and then wait until morning.
I have trouble staying asleep, or I wake early.	**Sleep when you feel tired:** Only try to sleep when you feel sleepy rather than spending hours lying awake in bed.
	Get up and try again later: Get up if you are still awake after around 20 minutes and do something calming or boring like sitting in a dimly lit room. Return to bed when you feel sleepy and try to sleep again. Repeat the process if you still can't sleep.
	Only use your bed for sleep and rest: Have a separate desk or work area, and keep phones and computers out of the bedroom, if possible.
I have trouble waking up, or I wake up exhausted.	**Get out in daylight:** Daylight helps create a sleep rhythm. Try to be outdoors when it's light for 30 minutes per day, especially mornings.
	Stick to your usual routine: Get up even if you are tired. Try a refreshing shower or a gentle stretch to liven you up.
	Regular physical activity keeps your body healthy and often helps more with tiredness than worrying about sleep.
Worries, anxious thoughts or memories keep me awake	**Write down your worries** in a journal or notebook at night if you wake up. Then put the book aside and tell yourself you will deal with it in the morning. Take a look at Chapter 7 on worry for ideas on how to do this.
	Use problem-solving when thinking about any worries during the day. Write your ideas down and take action for practical ways to cope. For a reminder of how to do this, turn to Chapter 5.
	You can't force yourself to sleep! Worrying about it will make you stressed and keep you awake longer. A night with less sleep is not a disaster. Try to accept it and focus on ways to take care of yourself the next day.

Do This  **10 Minutes**

Next steps for better sleep...

What are your next steps to create healthy sleep habits?	
What small changes might help improve your sleep routine? This could be anything from increasing your daytime physical activity to planning a calming bedtime routine where you put your phone out of sight and relax in a warm bath each evening.	

Kanye says: I had a bad habit of looking at social media late in the evening and I would always see something that made me feel anxious and kept me awake. I started putting my phone downstairs well before bedtime so I was less tempted to check it. It also helped me to go out with my dad to walk the dog in the evening. I could talk to him about some of my worries, and this made me feel a bit better. If I wake up with worries in the night, I've been writing them down and telling myself that I'll deal with them the next day. When I read the journal in the morning, it's usually something that's no big deal anyway! My sleep still isn't perfect, but it feels better than before.

Physical activity

Physical activity has many health benefits. It can strengthen your muscles and bones, help you to keep a healthy weight and reduce the risk of many illnesses such as heart problems, cancer and diabetes.

Physical activity can also reduce anxiety and improve your emotional wellbeing. Being active leads to the release of 'feel-good' hormones which make you calmer and happier. It increases your energy levels and can reduce feelings of stress, irritability and worry. Regular daytime activity can improve your sleep. It is also very social and can be a great way to develop friendships and connect with others through a shared interest.

Carrying out exercise can create a sense of achievement and is a way to develop and improve skills that build your confidence and self-esteem. Being active is also a great way to strengthen your concentration, memory and thinking skills. You can use short bursts of activity to break up long periods of studying or sitting.

 Pause and Think   **10 Minutes**

Different types of physical activity

Different people enjoy different types of physical activity. It's important to look for things that you enjoy or ways to calm an active mind. You can also find ways to bring more movement into your daily routine and reduce time spent staying still.

Types of physical activity	Does this interest you?	What could be the next step? How can you bring this into your life?
Walking, hiking or increasing your daily step count		
Cycling, jogging or athletics		
Yoga, Pilates, martial arts or dance		
Jumping on a trampoline		
Skateboarding, ice-skating or rollerblading		
Strength training, going to the gym or circuit training		
Swimming or any kind of water sport		

Ball sports such as football, rugby, netball or basketball		
Outdoor activities such as climbing, canoeing or paddle boarding		
Physical work such as gardening or working outside		
What other types of activity can you include?		

Physical activity and anxiety

Making regular physical activity one of your Healthy Life Habits is a really important way to reduce feelings of anxiety and worry. Look at the following ways to use physical activity to improve your mental health.

Physical activity habits	How could you use this tip? What will you do differently?
Create a regular routine: Make time for physical activity as an essential part of life by including it in your daily or weekly routine. Can you combine being active with something you already do such as walking to school or work, or going straight to a sports club on your way home?	
Use activity to calm your active mind: Physical activity can help to discharge stress and anxiety and leave you feeling calmer and with a mind that is more settled and less active. What types of activity work best for you? Would you prefer a peaceful solo swim or a jog, or the chance to walk and talk with a close friend?	

cont.

213

Physical activity habits	How could you use this tip? What will you do differently?
Make it social: Exercising with friends helps with motivation and enjoyment and can build your confidence in social situations. Who can you enlist to go for a walk, join you at the gym or in a dance class? Can you join an outdoor activity group such as Scouts or Guides? Do you like team sports?	
Make it fun: Think of ways to make getting active more enjoyable. Can you plan a fun day out with friends? Would you prefer increasing your step count while window shopping in your local town, taking your dog for a walk, learning a new dance routine or going geocaching?	
Start low and go slow: If you are not currently very active, aim for realistic small goals. What might be a micro-step to get you moving, even for a few minutes each day? Even sitting less is a start. A 10-minute walk can slowly build up to a jog, and you can gradually increase the speed and distance. Avoid over-ambitious targets that put you off getting started.	
Setbacks are normal! Don't let these throw you permanently off track. On a busy week or if you are tired or injured, cut down your activity levels but try not to stop completely. Start building up again gradually when you are ready.	

 **Do This**  **10 Minutes**

Next steps for physical activity habits...

What are your next steps to create healthy activity habits?	
What small changes might help to overcome your anxiety with regular physical activity, sport, exercise or movement? Can you commit to planning a few small changes over the next week?	

 Read This **10 Minutes**

Healthy technology habits

Your technology habits can also affect your emotions and mood. Living in a digital age brings many advantages, but it can also be hard to keep track of or control how much time you are spending online. Overuse of technology or screens can affect your productivity and memory, trigger anxiety, dampen creative thinking and affect your sleep.

Technology use can become a problem if it's getting in the way of other important life activities, such as reducing your focus on other important tasks or distracting you when talking or listening to other people. Too much screen time also stops you from being physically active, and reading negative news stories or constantly comparing yourself with others on social media can increase your anxiety and lower your mood and confidence.

The aim is to balance your use of technology with other important parts of life, following your Guide as you make wise choices about how to use your time. Using a screen time tracker can help you record how much time you are spending on a phone, tablet or computer so you can decide if your patterns of screen use are slipping into unhealthy habits.

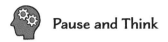 **Pause and Think**  **10 Minutes**

What are your technology habits?

How much time each day or week do you spend using technology or online? Complete the table below:

Technology habits	How many hours each day or week?
Working or studying online	
Using social media	
Playing computer games	
Sending messages or pictures to others	
FaceTime or video calls	
Other types of technology	

Now ask yourself:

What do you notice in your technology habits? Is technology contributing positively to your mood or self-esteem?	
Do your technology habits cause a distraction or get in the way of other important parts of life?	
Do you use technology to avoid difficult feelings such as anxiety or worry?	
Do you need to make any changes in your technology habits? What might be the first step?	

216

Drugs and alcohol

Drug and alcohol problems can cause physical and emotional damage. If you are affected, it's important to recognize the problem and seek help. We recommend that you talk to a trusted adult or your doctor if these have become an issue for you.

Summary: Healthy Life Habits for anxiety

→ You can improve feelings of anxiety and worry by creating Healthy Life Habits which include your sleep, physical activity and eating patterns.

→ It's also important to cut back on unhealthy choices such as smoking, drinking alcohol and using drugs, or overuse of technology or screens.

→ If you prioritize and repeat healthy actions and choices, they will become part of your routine.

Final thoughts

Make a note of anything you have found helpful, interesting or surprising from this chapter.

....

....

....

....

....

....

What are you going to do now? Can you choose one small action for the coming week based on what you have read so far?

....

....

....

....

....

References

James, A.C., Reardon, T., Soler, A., James, G. and Cresswell, G. (2020) 'Cognitive behavioural therapy for anxiety disorders in children and adolescents.' *Cochrane Database Syst Rev. 11*, 11, doi: 10.1002/14651858. CD013162.pub2.

The Prince's Trust (2021) *The Prince's Trust Tesco Youth Index 2021*. London: The Prince's Trust. https://documents.princes-trust.org.uk/Document_Tesco-Youth-Index-2021.pdf

van Dis, E.A.M, van Veen, S.C., Hagenaars, M.A., Batelaan, N.M., Bockting, C.L.H., van den Heuvel, R.M., Cuijpers, P.and Engelhard, I.M. (2020) 'Long-term outcomes of cognitive behavioural therapy for anxiety-related disorders: A systematic review and meta-analysis.' *JAMA Psychiatry 77*, 3, 265–273, doi: 10.1001/jamapsychiatry.2019.3986.

Finding Support

Here are some useful organizations you can turn to for support:

UK websites

Childline: If you are under 19 you can confidentially call, chat online or email about any problem, big or small: www.childline.org.uk

Cruse: Offering support, advice and information to children, young people and adults when someone dies: www.cruse.org.uk

Harmless: Provides support, information, training and consultancy to people who self-harm, their friends and families, and professionals: www.harmless.org.uk

NHS Better Health – every mind matters: www.nhs.uk/every-mind-matters/lifes-challenges

Papyrus: Confidential advice and support for young people struggling with suicidal thoughts or anyone concerned that a young person could be thinking of suicide: www.papyrus-uk.org

Report Abuse to CEOP: Child exploitation and online protection website run by the National Crime Agency to enable young people to report sexual and other forms of online abuse: www.ceop.police.uk/safety-centre

Samaritans: Whatever you're going through, at any age, you can contact the Samaritans for support and help in a crisis: www.samaritans.org

Shout: If you are a young person struggling to cope, text YM to 85258 for free, 24/7 support.

The Mix: Online information and a helpline for under-25s offering support for anything troubling you: www.themix.org.uk

Young Minds: UK charity fighting for children and young people's mental health: www.youngminds.org.uk

US and international websites

988 Suicide and Crisis Lifeline: Free and confidential support for people in distress or crisis via text, phone or online chat: www.988lifeline.org

Active Minds: Nonprofit organization supporting mental health awareness and education for young adults: www.activeminds.org

Crisis Text Line: A free 24/7 texting service for young people and adults that can connect you with a trained crisis counsellor: www.crisistextline.org

Mental Health America: Nonprofit organization dedicated to promoting mental health, wellbeing and preventing illness: www.mhanational.org/childrens-mental-health

My Life Is Worth Living: Animated online stories focusing on teen characters overcoming emotional challenges such as depression, cyberbullying and fear of disappointing others: https://mylifeisworthliving. org

National Alliance on Mental Illness (NAMI): Resources, information and support for teenagers and young adults dealing with mental health issues: www.nami.org/Your-Journey/Kids-Teens-and-Young-Adults

The Trevor Project: Provides crisis support for LGBTQ+ young people by phone and text, as well as information and an international community: www.thetrevorproject.org